PE🌐PLE
FIRST™

Books by Jack Lannom

Untapped Potential – Turning Ordinary People Into Extraordinary Performers

The Leader's Leader

Quantum Mind Learning Series

Memory Genius Learning Series

You are a Genius Children's Learning Software

Remembering Names and Faces

People First Book Series
1. *People First: Building Lives and Passing on a Legacy*

Forthcoming:

2. *People First: Achieving Balance in an Unbalanced World*
3. *People First: Raising "People First" Kids*
4. *People First: Releasing the Genius in You*
5. *People First: The Power of Giving*
6. *People First: Developing Physical Intelligence*
7. *People First: Building Relationship Power*
8. *People First: People First for Teens*
9. *People First: Sifu's Mentorship Secrets*
10. *People First: Sifu's Wealth Building Secrets*

PE●PLE
FIRST™

Building Lives
And
Passing on a Legacy

By
Jack Lannom

For information about special discounts for bulk purchases, please contact:
Lannom Incorporated, fax to: 954-392-1533, or:
Debbie@jacklannom.com
www.jacklannom.com

Book cover design by Chris Bongart
Book interior design by Cheryl Philips

Lannom Incorporated
#222
2114 North Flamingo Road
Pembroke Pines, Florida 33028

Library of Congress control number: 2005902872

ISBN 0-9766671-0-X (Hard back)

Dedication

How did Republic Services, Inc. -- with 13,400 dedicated people in 21 states -- go from having annual revenue of $40 million in 1996 to more than $2.7 billion today and become one of the Best Managed Service Companies in North America according to Forbes magazine?

Jim O'Conner, *Chairman and CEO of Republic Services, learned a successful business secret from his friend and former boss, H. Wayne Huizenga. The four-fold strategic system is: (1) dedication to people (2) a focus on execution (3) proper cash management and (4) strategic growth and acquisitions.*

The order of this business initiative is very significant because it places people first as a fundamental starting point for success and long-term viability. It is no surprise to learn that Republic's slogan in 2005 is, "A Company that Cares."

It is my honor to dedicate this book to Republic Services, Inc. -- a company that embodies the principles of People First. From the CEO to the men and women in the field who faithfully serves the customer – Republic Services is truly a company that cares!

Testimonials

"People First" is an outstanding contribution to the literature in the leadership field! The book is "content filled" and "reader friendly"! I am a Professor in Marketing at the University of Illinois at Chicago. I have reviewed many books on leadership. People First presents a compelling statement focused on empowering people through systematic building of interpersonal relationships. At the University of Illinois at Chicago, I am teaching the People First principles to my students. I teach the concepts of "The Pyramid of People Power", "MMFI–Make Me Feel Important", "Create a Culture of Recognition and Celebration"...and many others. The People First text clearly presents specific "hands-on" techniques that can build a powerful leadership style for the reader. As a consultant and professional educator in the network marketing industry, I am strongly endorsing People First as "required reading" in relationship building to my company clients and network marketing distributor audiences worldwide. I look forward to reading the other books in the People First series and sharing the philosophy. You have written a winner, Jack. Congratulations!
– Charles W. King, Professor of Marketing, University of Illinois at Chicago
Co-Founder, Faculty Administrator and Seminar Leader
of the UIC Certificate Seminar in Network Marketing
Researcher, Educator, Author and Consultant in Network Marketing

As a "Company that Cares", Republic Servics understands that value of our people and the critical role that they play in our success. Both individually and collectively, we want people to believe in themselves and to become more passionate about everything they do. This book provides a simple yet powerful message regarding the importance of caring for yourself, your family, your co-workers and your customers. People First is a road map to follow if you care and want to create a great place to work.

I highly recommend People First.
– James E. O'Connor, Chairman & CEO Republic Services, Inc.
Rated as one of America's Top 100 CEO's

If you truly care about real success, which is honoring and enhancing the unlimited potential of others, Jack Lannom's "People First" is a must read. This unique and inspiring story teaches you how to make a difference in your own life by making a difference in the lives of others. To read it is to be inspired. To study and apply it can change your life forever.
– Jack Maitland, Former Running Back, Baltimore Colts & New England
Patriots, President, Maitland, Inc., Creative Marketing Specialists

After a recent introduction to Jack Lannom, I was asked to read an advance copy of "People First". As I did so, it occurred to me that if I wanted to prosper in my business, I must treat my talented team members (Purpose Partners) with the exalted dignity and worth that they deserve. I must seek to find the exalted potentiality in each of them as we hire, train, and seek to retain and advance them in their chosen fields. Otherwise I should expect to join the ranks of those businesses whose growth is hindered by a failure to retain qualified workers when they depart to go work for someone who does honor and respect them. I encourage every business leader to read this book. Carefully consider it's message and apply the wisdom it contains in developing a People First *philosophy in their workplace. Congratulations, Jack on writing the next great guidebook to success in business.*
– Scott A. Dennison, CEO/Founder, Inspired Life Development

Testimonials

"People First" was an engaging, entertaining, and powerful read. I want all of my energy consultants – and all my friends – to read this book! It's too easy in this fast-paced, high-tech world to forget what truly matters: the celebration of our collective human spirit.
– Sy Richardson, CEO of Krystal Planet

Great reading. I have really enjoyed the refreshment. Put to work immediately for my own life. Thanks a million!!!!! A work such as this is something to be truly proud of and I am proud of you for being able to write such a masterpiece. I am honored that you have chosen me to be a part of your work. Please let me know how I can be of continued assistance.
– Sy Richardson, CEO, Five Star Telecom

I must say that "People First" is one of, if not the best book, I have ever read. It was a fun read and once started, hard to put down. Your story applies the simple principles of loving each other first and foremost as taught by our Creator. Many people seem to forget what really matters once they start down that path toward success, and then wonder why they often hit speed bumps that slow them down along the way.

I believe that if everyone were taught to utilize these principles within the "pyramid of people power" in grade school, we could eventually eliminate crime. Becoming a "success" would ultimately take on new meaning.

I love the idea of the shirt stating "under construction" and hope you do not mind if I find a way to use that phrase as we build our company in the context of how you used it. Also, the coin allowing permission to either fail or succeed. Brilliant! I noticed that you used the phrase "untapped potential" at least three times that I counted.

Thank you. I loved the message and am proud to call you my friend.
– Chuck Simpson, CEO, Amerikare

The book is a great read (I read it in two sittings)! I think America is hungry for this type of message. The book is a great read because you made it a story about specific people and not simply principles and beliefs. You put faces and emotions behind these principles and beliefs.

Today's corporate world has its priorities completely backwards. Explaining that 'Once we get our financial balance sheet in order, THEN, we might have time for initiatives like 'People First''. Rather than realizing that by putting 'People First', the balance sheet will follow. The leaders need to be strong enough to have faith in the employees to do the right thing, while the employees simply want to do the right thing, and get a little recognition for it.

The challenges will be:
1) Get the 'Top Dog' (Dan Burton) completely on board. This has to be top down and all eyes will be on the 'Boss' to see if he's 'doing' or just 'talking'. The first sign of the 'Boss' just 'talking' the beliefs, but acting otherwise, the movement immediately breaks down. 2) There is healthy skepticism among employees due to the challenge #1 listed above. Most corporations have 'rolled out' numerous 'initiatives' that go nowhere due to lack of follow-thru from leadership and employees therefore, have built up a guard of skepticism.

I look forward to the book hitting the stores in the US and recommending it to my business associates. For the committed, conducting business in a manner that puts 'People First' could be the best business decision they ever make.
– Mike Kiernan, Maverick Oil Company

Testimonials

I am involved in the training industry that impacts many industries. The most successful companies are in a constant state of helping personal growth develop from the owner all the way to the person who started with the company yesterday. I will recommend "People First" to every one of my clients and also suggest that they do as I have, and pass it on to every member of their family! "People First" is not a "how to" it's a "why" for life. I am certain that it will become a classic!
— George Madiou, President/CEO, LiveOnlineMeeting.com

I have just finished reading your book "People First", it was a great pleasure. I have read several thousands of self-help books through 30 years and I am not easily impressed. However, your book did impress me, here are the reasons:

1. *It was well written and had a very nice story with a happy ending. (I had tears in my eyes at the end)*
2. *It was easy reading.*
3. *It WILL help a lot of people, not only in their jobs but also at home in the family.*
4. *The "people first philosophy" will catch on like wild fire (it will be like Dale Carnegie's "How to Win Friends")*
5. *The book will be bought by management and given to employees ... oops ... purpose partners.*
6. *Trainers all over the world WILL "steal" and start using "the Pyramid of People Power" by Jack Lannom in their trainings, like "Maslow's pyramid". (In fact Jack, I have already used your pyramid in Norwegian in some of my seminars because I got it some time back in e-mail Newletter from someone in USA, and I did not know that you where the one that made it).*

Jack, your book will be a fantastic success, I am sure about it and I am proud to know you, and even better, work with you in coming years. By the way, I have a friend who has translated and published many books among the "Who Moved My Cheese" here in Norway, maybe he/we could get the right to publish it here.
— Rino Solberg, Chairman/Editor-in-Chief, Success Magazine in Uganda

Your book, People First, is so full of multidimensional phrases, ideas, and achievement formulas formatted in such a way that once the reader has read the lines, it is learned! You have demonstrated incomparably that, as one of your passages reflects, every human being has exalted worth and potential, and are marvels of creation!

Motivating and teaching to unlock powers within, achieve highest potential, and implementing techniques in putting People First *~ while working together making needed differences ~ while uplifting, facilitating and expressing our human spirit! ... all ... is in your* People First Program!

We all thank you! for "celebrating the human spirit" the way you do ~ in your 'great' writings, and inspirational in person events!
— Keith Colley, Founder/Producer/Writer, www.candoproject.com

Table of Contents

Prologue:
A Call for Help

*A*s Dan Burton pulls his car out of the executive parking lot on a Tuesday night. He is deeply troubled. His face is drawn down into what is becoming a perpetual frown. However, it is time to leave the office to go to his weekly Walu Kung Fu class, and Dan actually brightens a bit. His schedule doesn't leave time for many outside activities, but Dan strives never to miss this class. The physical activity is wonderful, and during the hour-and-a-half he spends with Sifu Li, the Grandmaster who owns and operates the school, Dan is able to escape the nagging, wearisome questions that have been plaguing him every day.

Sifu (pronounced "See foo," which means "teacher" in Chinese) is one of those "special" people: a man with sparkling eyes, a smile that never fades, and what appears to be a genuine and abounding love for all of his students. Dan has been attending Sifu Li's Walu Kung Fu school for six years, and he is convinced that this is no mere "appearance"—Sifu's appreciation for his students is sincere. He always has an encouraging word and patient instruction for even the most awkward student, and his gentle spirit, self-deprecating humor, and unfailing courtesy and wisdom are a constant source of delight.

Dan smiles to himself as he recalls how cautiously he initially approached the Walu Kung Fu school. He had heard somewhere that most martial arts teachers seek to inculcate their students with the doctrines of eastern religion, which Dan was certain would clash with the beliefs he had held ever since he was a boy. However, a coworker who attended the school assured Dan that, far from being a proponent of eastern mysticism, Sifu Li taught timeless moral principles along with the practical techniques of the martial arts. Today Dan would readily admit that he has grown to respect Sifu more than any man he knows, and he is not alone in that regard. During the six years that Dan has attended the school, it has doubled in size. Yet Sifu never seems preoccupied by "business."

Dan arrives just as workouts begin, and takes his place with the other students doing their stretching and warm-ups. Sifu's bright brown eyes are scanning the room, making sure his students are limbering up properly, and for a moment his eyes meet Dan's. Sifu's face lights with a warm smile, and he nods a greeting. Dan smiles back, and suddenly a thought comes to him: *Why don't you ask Sifu to give you some advice about your problem?* Dan is startled at the idea. *Oh, come on, get real*, he tells himself. *I'm the CEO of a multi-million dollar firm, and Sifu just teaches Kung Fu*—the internal argument dies abruptly. Dan nods to himself as he quickly acknowledges that Sifu is more than "just" a teacher. His school—Sifu calls it a *kwoon*, Chinese for "school" or "training room"—is a massive success by anyone's standards. Sifu has earned international recognition as a Grandmaster—an undefeated world champion in international sparring and forms competitions. He is, quite simply, one of the most accomplished practitioners of Walu Kung Fu in the world.

However, Sifu is not only a man skilled with his fists and feet, he is also an extremely successful businessman. More than 500 students are enrolled in the school that Dan attends, and thousands of students attend nearly one hundred Sifu Li Walu Kung Fu schools across the nation, as well as two large facilities in Europe. Sifu has made investments, he owns commercial property, and Dan has had occasion to visit his palatial, 10,000-square-foot home.

Sifu can help you, Dan, that inner voice insists. *And have you ever known him to turn down someone who asked him for help?* Dan nods again, thinking that he has never met a man more generous in his spirit than

Sifu. *Okay*, Dan tells himself, *I'll speak to Sifu after class*. Almost immediately, Dan feels better, and he quickly forgets the problems that have been troubling him for the past several months. He immerses himself so completely in the night's training that he is surprised to hear Sifu say, "Thank you, students, that will be all for tonight."

Dan joins a line of people who are waiting to speak to Sifu. Most of the questions concern a particular move or energy principle, and Sifu cheerfully answers every question, often taking time to demonstrate the actual move that the student should make and asking follow-up questions to make sure that the student has truly grasped the lesson to be learned. The rest of the group watches with rapt attention. No one minds waiting in line to speak to Sifu, because they often learn a great deal from watching his instruction of others. Finally, it is Dan's turn.

Dan approaches Sifu and gives a two-handed salute, as is the custom of the school to show respect for the teacher. Sifu's face cracks into a smile, but Dan can see that Sifu's eyes are searching his own. "Ah, Dan," Sifu says warmly. "Are you well?"

Dan automatically starts to answer with a meaningless affirmative, then checks himself: "I'm doing fine—well, actually, Sifu, I've been dealing with some things at work lately... I, uh..." Dan hesitates, and his eyes shift away from Sifu's steady gaze. Dan is, after all, the CEO of a major firm; he is the guy everybody comes to for answers, and he is not at all accustomed to admitting any weakness or asking someone else for help. But he is reaching the point of desperation, and he forces himself to try again. When his eyes meet the teacher's, he sees no impatience there—only concern. "I've been going through some tough times, and I can't seem to find my way out, and I was hoping..." Once again, Dan's voice trails off.

"Perhaps I can be of some assistance?" asked Sifu Li gently. "Dan, there is an old proverb that states, 'When the student is ready, the teacher appears.'"

Dan nods gratefully, relieved. "Could I buy you breakfast one morning this week?"

Sifu nods quickly and grips Dan by the shoulder. "Tomorrow morning?" Dan quickly agrees, and the two men arrange the time and location.

The next morning, Dan arrives five minutes early for their appointment, determined not to keep Sifu waiting. He finds Sifu already seated at a table, sipping a glass of orange juice and chatting with the waitress, who is beaming with pleasure at whatever Sifu has just said to her.

As Dan slides into the booth, Sifu gestures toward the waitress and smiles. "Dan, I would like to introduce you to Cynthia. She was just telling me about her son's Little League team."

Dan is preoccupied with what he plans to tell Sifu, and nods a curt acknowledgment to the waitress and gives her his order. Sifu gives the waitress another wide smile. "Cynthia, it has been very pleasant to meet you and talk with you." Cynthia leaves, and Sifu turns his attention to Dan.

"Thank you for meeting with me, Sifu," Dan begins. "I know how busy you must be."

"I am never too busy to help one of my students," Sifu replies evenly. "I was getting ready to ask you to meet with me." Dan's face reveals his surprise. "The stress shows in your eyes, Dan," Sifu explains gently.

Dan feels an unexpected rush of emotion, and his voice sounds hoarse in his ears as his story comes pouring out in a sudden flood. "I don't ever remember feeling like this. I feel like my life is spinning out of control. I *know* my company is out of control...

"Sifu, there are men I know—men who work for me, men I play golf with, some of the men at the Walu Kung Fu School—who look at me and my life, and I'm sure they assume I'm a very happy and successful man." Dan's voice takes on a sarcastic tone. "After all, I'm the CEO of a multi-million-dollar retail firm which employs close to 1000 men and women. I'm in excellent health, I've got a lovely wife, and my children are both honors students and plan to attend prestigious universities. You'd think that a man like me shouldn't have any real worries, right? No worries?

"Well, it's all falling apart. My company has really been struggling. We've been steadily losing market share over the last few years. Not only that, but we monitor our customer satisfaction scores carefully, and those numbers are falling off dramatically. Oh, the company is still paying dividends, but earnings are down by more than half in the last three years. I've tried every solution I can think of: management shake-ups, layoffs, rebate programs, increasing our advertising budget... I even took our senior managers on a weekend retreat... but the numbers are continuing to slide.

"The bottom line is, our customers are going elsewhere to shop, and I'm certain it's because we don't have the right people in place to meet the customers' needs. But the new people we're bringing in aren't doing any better. I've hired expensive consultants to teach them the latest customer service techniques, and our service scores are *still* falling!"

The waitress has brought his food, but Dan hasn't even picked up his fork. Now he scowls down at the plate and pushes it away from him, as if the food smells badly. "Yesterday our CFO gave me the latest figures." Dan says exasperatedly. "Sifu, I've slashed our payroll and expenses to their lowest levels in years, but gross sales and net income are down *again*, and the latest responses to our customer satisfaction surveys show that our customers are more ambivalent about shopping with us than ever."

Dan looks up, almost angrily, at his teacher. "I felt sick to my stomach when I read that report! I've tried *everything!* Sifu, our company is fifty years old, and we've been in a steady growth mode—until now. The shareholders aren't going to wait much longer for me to get this thing turned around. Earnings are down, and they'll be looking for someone to blame it on. I need answers, and quick." Dan abruptly reaches out and pulls the plate of food toward him, but he makes no move to eat; he simply stares down at the food. Sifu waits in silence, sensing that there is more.

Dan looks up again, his eyes wide and pleading, almost child-like. "I've been working a *lot* of hours—a lot of hours—these last few years, you know, trying to get on top of this thing. At first, my wife used to complain about it. She said she wanted to spend more time with me. Now the only thing she says is that we're like two strangers living in the same house."

Dan's voice lowers. "And you know what? I think she's right. Both the kids are going away to college soon, and then it'll be just the two of us. I'm beginning to wonder if Cheryl and I ever had anything in common, other than the kids. Sifu... if I lose my job... I think Cheryl might leave me. But who knows?" Dan concludes miserably. "If I manage somehow to *keep* this job, she might leave!"

It is all out on the table now. There is just one last thing, yet it is perhaps the hardest for Dan to say. Sifu has to strain to hear the last words, almost a whisper: "I don't know what to do."

People First

Sifu sits in silence for what seems like a long time. Dan waits, fighting against impatience. Finally he can bear it no longer. "So what do you think?" he asks abruptly.

Sifu smiles at Dan. "A man who speaks with mouthful gives listener earful," he replies in his soft voice. There is humor dancing in the older man's eyes, and Dan realizes that he has been gently admonished for not waiting for the teacher to speak. Suddenly the voice of Sifu Li, Grandmaster, comes back to Dan from his years of Walu Kung Fu training: "Be patient, watch your opponent, look for your opportunity. The fighter who rushes to attack without thought and study is often the one who loses." Dan makes a conscious effort to let the tension drain away.

As if sensing Dan's decision, Sifu begins to speak at that very moment, but only to ask Dan a seemingly unrelated question: "Dan, how did you hear about my *kwoon?*"

Dan cocks his head at Sifu. *What could this possibly have to do with my problems?* he wonders. "Well, a man who used to work for me told me about the school."

Sifu nods, his dark eyes sparkling with that gentle humor. "Richard Wiggins told you about us, yes?"

Once again, Dan mentally kicks himself. Sifu hadn't asked the question to acquire information, but to guide Dan's thinking. "Yes, Sifu," Dan replies humbly.

"How did Richard convince you to join us?"

This time, Dan considers before answering. "Well... someone told me that Richard had earned a black sash in the martial arts and won first-place in a regional tournament. When I learned that what other marital arts call a 'belt' is called a 'sash' in Kung Fu, I was impressed! Here's a guy who could snap me in half without breaking a sweat, yet he always seemed so... gentle. Richard was always very much in control, and he displayed such great humility. I was impressed by his personality, so one day I asked him about how he kept himself in check, and he said he'd learned it from his Grandmaster... you, Sifu.

Richard kept talking about how much he loved your school and the wisdom you impart to your students. I guess you could say that I saw a product of your work, Sifu, and I was impressed."

Sifu nods approvingly. "You have been with me six years now; you see how I run my *kwoon*. Have you noticed that I do not advertise? Others spend thousands of dollars in advertising, yet our schools are much more successful. What do you think is the reason?"

"You don't need to advertise because your students do it for you," Dan says promptly, "like the way Richard told me about you. There are at least forty people from my company alone who go to your school. They all heard about you from those of us who are already there."

Sifu nods and leans forward. Dan has grown familiar with the gesture over the years. Sifu is about to impart something important, and Dan has learned to listen with respect. "When I was preparing to open my first school," Sifu begins. "My Grandmaster told me that I must concentrate on becoming an exemplary model of the art of Kung Fu. When I had accomplished that, he said I must always put the students first, rather than simply looking to make a lot of money. If I did those two things, I would succeed."

Dan is a little puzzled. "Sifu, all your students know that you are a tremendous example of the art. We've watched you on television and seen you win international competitions. Now, I don't have international recognition, but I work very hard to set the right example for my people. I'm always the first to arrive at the office, and I'm usually the last to leave."

"Yes, Dan, but you are missing one very important point." Sifu's voice is very soft. Dan recognizes the tone. Sifu is at his most gentle when one of his students has performed poorly. "You have spoken about what you do, but it is very important to remember this: **Belief is the basis for behavior; attitude is the antecedent of action; philosophy is the precursor of performance.** You work very hard, Dan, but what are you working hard to accomplish?"

Dan answers automatically, "My job is to make our company profitable, so that it becomes attractive to investors. If they get a good return on their investment, they'll keep buying the stock. Then I make money, and everybody else makes money, and everyone is happy."

Sifu's voice is gentler still, and Dan begins to wonder what he is missing. "Dan," Sifu asks, "what would you say is the truth about who people really are?"

"The people who work for me are there to get a job done and earn a profit for the company," Dan responds. "I've made it very clear to everyone; they've got to perform in order to help me turn a profit for the shareholders."

"So... people are not first in your company?" Sifu asks. "Profits come first?"

Dan feels impatience returning. "Sifu, without profits I can't afford to *hire* any people!"

Sifu's smile never wavers, but Dan can hear a new note of authority in his voice. The Grandmaster is speaking. "You have a serious problem, my friend. I am willing to help you find the solution to your problem, but it will take some time to outline that solution. We may be sitting here for a few hours. Can you do that today?"

"Sifu, I have the time, but I don't understand why you're so sure you know what's wrong with our organization. What do you think is wrong?" Dan asks.

"You have dehumanized your company," Sifu replies implacably. "If you reevaluate your thinking about people, and humanize your company, you should find that the profits you seek will follow."

"You see, Dan," Sifu continues. "Before you begin to work hard, you must be sure you are working toward the right goal, yes? You must work smarter not harder." Dan nods, looking at Sifu curiously. "Before you concentrate on great performance, you must consider the philosophy that guides that performance. As I said, your beliefs guide the way you behave." Sifu looks directly into Dan's eyes. "You have bad beliefs about people, Dan. As a result you—and the people around you—are behaving badly, and your company is performing poorly."

Dan is abashed, but he feels compelled to defend himself. "Sifu, I treat my people very well. Our human resources department monitors compensation plans to be sure that we offer pay and benefits that are as good as anyone's—and better than most! We're careful to provide equal opportunities to women and minorities. We're a stable company with a good, clean working environment. What more am I supposed to do for them? How can you say I have bad beliefs about people?"

"Simply put Dan, you are merely functional and not personal. Now let me give you some words which my Sifu gave me when I first started my apprenticeship: **Truth in all things, wisdom in all things, excellence in all things.** Would you say those are good words to live by?"

"Of course," Dan replies. "There is no quality of life without them. I guess the deeper thought is, try to live your life without truth, wisdom and excellence."

"Good! So let us discuss the truth about who people are. Do you remember our interaction with Cynthia?"

Dan looks at Sifu blankly. He cannot think of anyone he knows named Cynthia.

"Our waitress, Dan," Sifu reminds him. "Did you notice how she was smiling when you entered the restaurant this morning? That is because I honored her. Dan, people like people who like them first. I was truly interested to learn who she is and what makes her happy. I took the initiative. Why do I treat her that way? Because she is a human being! *Every* human being has exalted dignity, exalted worth, and exalted potential. Cynthia is a walking miracle; she is a marvel of creation; and she is made in God's image.

"Dan, when you sat down in this booth, I observed your interaction with her. There was none! You stared at your menu; you did not look her in the eye even once. You did not acknowledge her in any way, except to tell her what you wanted from her. That is a close encounter of the *impersonal* kind. When I met Cynthia, I asked for her name and used it, I talked to her, and I learned about who she is. I received her, I engaged her, and I celebrated her. I treated her as a valuable individual. She does not have to guess how I feel about her; she can tell by the way I treat her. Watch how she serves me while we are here; she works willingly, and with passion. She is operating in excellence. I have helped to elicit that excellence because I live in celebration—the celebration of the human spirit.

"There is no such thing as 'Big "I," little "you"' in my world, Dan. Each individual is important; everyone should be treated with honor and respect. I believe Corporate America has forgotten the truth about what it means to be human." Sifu smiles again to take the sting from his next words: "I am afraid you may have forgotten, my friend."

Dan opens his mouth to object, then closes it again and drops his eyes from Sifu's steady gaze. *He may be right*, Dan tells himself.

"We have talked about truth in all things," Sifu continues softly. "The next point is wisdom in all things. Wisdom means the skillful application of knowledge. You know that from your martial arts training, Dan. Kung Fu is all about the *wise* application of force and leverage in the proper spot, yes? **A man or woman in business must focus energy and attention on people first—not profits first.** This is wisdom. The people in your organization are your most valuable asset. They are the ones who will earn the profits—if they perform with excellence and passion."

Dan shakes his head. "But Sifu, you don't understand my situation," he objects. "My people aren't loyal to me. I have to stand over the employees all the time and tell 'em what to do; otherwise they don't work. There's got to be hierarchy and control, or nothing gets done."

"I agree, Dan, there must be subordination in *all* aspects of life—in family and everywhere else—but it must be a *functional* subordination, not a subordination of human worth. Each member of the family—and each member of your organization, Dan—is valuable to the overall system. The contributions of each member are considered to have immense value, because each member is contributing to the success of the organization.

"Dan, you refer to the men and women on your staff as 'my people' and 'employees.' Would it not be better to call them 'Purpose Partners'? Do they not all share with you in the purpose of making your business successful? Are they not your partners in accomplishing that goal?"

"That's just it, Sifu," Dan grumbles. "Most of the time it seems like their purpose is just to put in time and pick up a paycheck. It's like they could care less about serving the customers!"

Suddenly Sifu's eyes are very bright. "Listen to me, Dan." For the first time, there is something like urgency in his voice. "If you hear nothing else I say, then hear me now: ***The men and women who work for you cannot impart what they do not possess!*** You have a bad belief about people; therefore your staff does not exhibit good behavior.

"Dan, the best philosophy is the precursor of the best perform-ance. You want to change the behavior of your staff without talking about your philosophy. Your beliefs should set people free to be them-selves and encourage them to tap into their potential to its fullest. Your philosophy should dictate the recognition and celebration of the human spirit. Every day at work should be a day of celebration for every member of your staff."

Sifu is interrupted by Cynthia's cheerful query: "Would you gentlemen like some more coffee?" During the exchange, Dan makes a conscious effort to look into her eyes and smile, and he realizes that Sifu was right; Dan is looking into the eyes of a complete stranger. He had not so much as glanced at her when she took his breakfast order.

When Cynthia has filled their cups and departed, Dan looks humbly back at Sifu. "But how do I do what you're saying? Make every day a day of celebration?"

"You create an environment of recognition and celebration by putting people first," Sifu replies. He sips his steaming coffee and smiles with pleasure. "**The philosophy is People First—whatever you want your customers to feel, your staff must feel it first!** When you do this, you will be practicing truth in all things, and wisdom in all things, and this kind of leadership produces a legacy of excellence. Excellence is the inevitable outcome of this philosophy. People will work in excellence when they are being treated excellently! And with the excellence will come the profits you seek. Profits are the spiritual and monetary outcomes of operating a business in truth, wisdom, and excellence. "

Dan is unconvinced. "Sifu, I'm grateful to you for making time to meet me this morning. But I came to talk to you about my business, not about philosophy."

"Dan, the practice of every thing is the practice of some philosophy," Sifu replies, unperturbed. "When you walked into this restaurant, I introduced you to Cynthia, and you immediately put your philosophy about people on display for all to see. You demonstrated that people are not very important to you. Yet you expect your Purpose Partners to demonstrate that your customers are very important to them! How do you expect your Purpose Partners to value what has not been modeled for them? Dan, how much of your leadership style is worth modeling?"

Dan looks at Sifu wordlessly. He would like to argue..."*Bluster*" *would be a more accurate word,* he acknowledges wryly. *I've watched how Sifu treats his students for the last six years; I know I don't honor people the way Sifu does. I didn't even look at Cynthia! However, everything Sifu does in his relationships is worth modeling.*"

"Do you remember, Dan, the night at our *kwoon* when you first broke a board with your hand?"

Dan is jolted out of his thoughts. This, at least, is a happier subject. "You bet! I'll remember it for the rest of my life," he replies warmly. "I was pretty nervous, but you kept telling me you knew I could do it, and reminding me of all you'd taught me, and I broke it!"

"What exactly did I do?" Sifu prompts.

Dan smiles. "You led the whole class in a cheering session. Before I even broke the board, everyone was chanting 'Dan! Dan! Dan!' And then after I broke it, you grabbed me and hugged me..."—here Dan's voice softens—"...and there were tears in your eyes, Sifu." Dan looks at his teacher with wonder. "Breaking that board was the last test I had to pass in order to get the gold sash—my very first sash. You took the board I broke and signed it in front of everybody, and you personally tied the new sash around my waist. You handed me my certificate of accomplishment, displayed in a nice frame. My wife was there, and my children... and there were tears in my eyes at that point... I'll never forget it."

"We celebrated you, Dan," Sifu nods. "We honored you."

"Yes?"

"Now let me ask you, Dan; how much celebration takes place at your company?"

"What do you mean?" Dan asks.

"When an individual or group achieves small, incremental accomplishments, do you celebrate them?"

Dan hesitates, feeling trapped.

"You, personally, Dan?" Sifu persists. "Do you celebrate your Purpose Partners?"

Dan's eyes drop. "No," he says quietly. "No, Sifu, I don't celebrate them like you did for me... Personally? I don't celebrate them at all."

Sifu's voice is very gentle. "Dan, if your customer satisfaction scores are low, I suspect that employee satisfaction is much lower."

Dan nods an unhappy acknowledgment, his eyes still downcast.

"And if employee satisfaction is only thirty or forty per cent," Sifu continues inexorably, "how can you possibly expect customer satisfaction to be 100 percent? Or even seventy-five per cent? You cannot impart what you do not possess.

"Dan, my Sifu told me to concentrate on celebrating my students, *all* their little accomplishments, and sharing all their joy. He told me, 'Do not wait for them to get their black sash; you will be waiting for years to celebrate them!' He said that when the students break that first little board, no one should celebrate more than the teacher. And as the students move on to the more advanced sashes, the teacher should be the one who takes the greatest joy in their accomplishments and lets that joy show.

"Dan, I work to create a culture of transformation at all my kwoons. Students enter our schools and we start them on a transformational learning journey through a culture which tells them, 'I mean you no harm.' It is **not a critical culture, but one of recognition and celebration**, a culture which encourages them to reach for their highest and their best, not their lowest and least."

Sifu pauses and looks quizzically at Dan, a slight smile tugging at the corner of his mouth. "Dan, do you believe we have succeeded in creating such a culture in our *kwoon*?"

Dan nods without hesitation. "Yes, Sifu, you sure have."

"Dan, what happens when I walk into the *kwoon*?"

Dan's face brightens. "The room lights up when you walk into it, Sifu. We're happy to see you."

"Why?"

"Because you do all the things you're talking about," Dan replies. "You're a tenth degree black sash, a Grandmaster of Walu Kung Fu and a world champion, but you don't put us down when we make mistakes. The focus in the school is not all about you; it's all about us. We're on the learning journey together. You teach us and encourage us and celebrate us. Sifu, you must know that every one of your students loves you and would do anything for you."

Sifu smiles and nods in acknowledgment of Dan's praise. "Dan, have you developed a culture of recognition and celebration in your company?"

Dan had forgotten about his situation for a moment, and his face falls. *You've got to be honest*, he tells himself grimly. "No, Sifu," he admits. "Most of the conversation I have with my people is to tell them what they've done wrong."

"We work hard, very hard in our *kwoon*," Sifu continues. "We train hard, we sweat, but we have a lot of fun, too, yes? We celebrate each other, we build each other up, and we see people performing incredible feats, things they had never dreamed they could do. Dan, do the people who work for you have fun? Do they enjoy being part of your organization?"

"Sifu, I... No, Sifu, I don't suppose they do."

Sifu nods, and his voice is very gentle. "Dan, have you ever met a leader that the room lights up, glows, radiates.... when he walks out of the room?"

Dan is afraid to hear what is coming next, but he nods silently.

"Dan, are you a leader like that?"

Dan cannot meet his teacher's eyes. "Yes, Sifu, I expect that I am."

The silence at the table is leaden. Then Dan looks up, and there is a new light in his eyes. It may not be hope, but there is a spark of interest—a desire to hear more. "Sifu, you're saying I should run my business the same way you run your *kwoon*?"

"Precisely the same way."

"But Sifu, I'm a businessman; don't you believe that a major retail establishment should be run differently from a martial arts school?"

Sifu senses that Dan is not arguing so much as he is asking for more information, and he smiles with delight at Dan's question. "Do you not believe that I am a businessman, Dan? And am I wrong in thinking that you are a teacher?"

Dan's face flushes slightly. "Sifu, I know you're a very successful businessman. And I've *tried* to teach my people how to do better; they just aren't responding."

Sifu nods approvingly. "That is very good, Dan, you *should* be working to be a model and a mentor for your Purpose Partners. Look at it this way. You are one of the finest students I have ever instructed. You wear the black sash, and you have won regional tournaments. Why do you think you have done so well? I submit that you have flourished because I have a theory about people—I believe each one of my students possesses exalted worth, exalted dignity, and exalted potential. All they need is a leader and a mentor who believes in them more than they believe in themselves. The culture I maintain in our *kwoon* is a culture based on my beliefs about people, and this culture has allowed you to fully tap your potential. When you walked away from the tournaments carrying the first place trophy, did you believe that was the outcome of you being the very best fighter in your division? Or did you view yourself as the product of the best philosophy that was represented at the tournament?"

Dan looks at his teacher for a moment. "I always believed that I had worked hard, and that you were a tremendous teacher," he admits frankly. "I never gave any thought to a philosophy. I'm afraid I still don't quite understand what you are trying to tell me."

"Do you think you would have performed as well if I believed

I was the only one with special gifts?" Sifu asks. "What if I believed that you and all the other students were clumsy and slow, and that none of you would ever learn? Do you think you would have grown so quickly or so well?" Sifu shakes his head emphatically. "I am certain that *all* our students would be floundering if I didn't cherish the belief that human beings possess a shoreless, bottomless repository of talent and potential. The extraordinary performance that you have displayed, Dan, is a reflection of the philosophy that we have at our *kwoon*."

"I never thought about it that way," Dan says thoughtfully. "When I first came to your school, I saw your speed and balance, your concentration and flexibility, your incredible strength, and I wondered if you were from another planet! It didn't even occur to me that six years later I'd be doing many of the things I saw you do." That same curious light is still bright in Dan's eyes. He thinks for a moment, then slowly asks, "So... you're saying it's your *belief* about people that gave me the ability to win those tournaments and earn the black sash?" He is looking intently at his teacher. "I have to admit that I'm still struggling to accept the idea that people will improve their performance just because I believe they will."

"Ah, Dan, you are coming closer, but you still don't see it all!" Sifu leans forward again, his eyes very bright. "They will perform in excellence when *they* believe that you care about them and celebrate them first! Dan, whatever you want to see grow in your team members, you must sow the seeds of that crop yourself. If you want loyalty, you must sow the seeds of loyalty first. If you want your team members to value your customers and listen to them, you must first value and listen to your team. *People first, Dan!* **If you want profits to grow, then grow people first.**

"It is true, Dan, that your business and mine are not the same, but the principles of good business are *always* the same! The values and philosophy we follow at our *kwoon* will make you a more effective leader and help you turn your company around.

"Here is another proverb for you to commit to memory, Dan: '**If your goal is for one year, plant wheat. If your goal is for ten years, plant trees. But if your goal is for a lifetime, plant people.**' I have seen that far too many businesses are focused on the short-term gain, rather than on long-term growth. I meet the executives, Dan! I work with them every day! They do not understand that successful business management is not a short sprint; it is a long-term marathon, and they must learn to condition their thinking in that way. I believe, Dan, far too many businesses are focused on earnings and expediency rather than on excellence and ethics."

Sifu pauses for another swallow of coffee and makes a sour face. The coffee has grown cold. He raises his eyes to look for the waitress, only to see her headed toward him, smiling, a steaming coffee pot in hand. Sifu smiles back at Cynthia. "Forgive me, Cynthia. A man who wishes to enjoy hot coffee must stop talking and start drinking!" Cynthia smiles back and pours him a fresh cup. Sifu enjoys a few sips of coffee before he begins to speak again.

"Dan, **Life is all about building strong, caring, trust-based, long-term relationships.** This is how you humanize your company. If the idea of growing people is not at the very center of your philosophy, your company has no soul. It is like a body without a spirit.

"Dan, it is an unhappy truth that many businesses sacrifice long-term partnerships on the altar of short-term profits. What the leaders fail to realize is that **profits are outcomes, not first principles.** Your first principles are your philosophy about people. Yes, it takes time to grow people and build relationships, but it pays off in a strong team of loyal Purpose Partners, long-lasting relationships, long-term profits, and a 'whatever-it-takes' mentality that thrives within the organization. The people in any company are a clear reflection of their leaders. Dispirited, dispassionate people are mirroring dispirited, dispassionate leadership."

Dan has been listening in respectful silence, but now he interrupts, almost wonderingly, "But Sifu, surely you don't think it's wrong for a business leader to do everything he can to make his business profitable! You want your franchises to be profitable, don't you?"

"Of course, my friend! I am not a wealthy philanthropist who no longer has to work for a living," Sifu grins. "I am a businessman who makes a living in the martial arts. I have built a multi-million dollar organization, with schools all over the United States, plus two more in Europe. When I tell you to put people first, I am not distinguishing between what is important and what is not important. Profits are essential for the success of my business. I use profits to buy the best equipment, to build new schools, and to provide the parties and celebrations we have for our students. Not only that, but I pay myself and my partners well. I want my partners to make a good living! So I need profits to stay in business and grow my business. But Dan, my focus cannot be on profits first, people second. **Profits are like food. You need profits to live, but they aren't what you live for.** That is the attitude to maintain if you wish to achieve consistent long-term success.

"Too many of the men and women I meet have money without meaning, cash without contentment, finances without fulfillment, prosperity without purpose, success without significance, and shadow without substance. They have acquired many *things*, Dan, but they have completely forgotten what is most important. People first, Dan. Profits are important; however, people are even more important. **Treat people like gold, and they'll shine like gold.**" Dan, you must make the decision today that no company will put people first more than you. In other words, no one will honor, value and celebrate people more than Dan Burton. Consequently, you will not only attract the best people, you will also keep the best people."

Dan has been focused intently on Sifu's every word. Now he shakes his head. "Sifu, you talk to us about these things during our Kung Fu classes, and I thought I had listened well and learned. Now I'm beginning to think I missed the whole point. You're telling me to apply these lessons in every aspect of my life—the personal and pro-fessional—not just to the martial arts! I've heard you say that to our class dozens of times... but somehow I never thought about applying your philosophy to my business. Sifu, I've been a fool!"

There is a new look in Sifu's eyes now, a look Dan has seen countless times during the past six years. When a student has demon-strated a new skill for the first time, the Grandmaster often appears to be even more delighted than the student—and that look of pure joy is shining in his eyes now. Sifu reaches across the table and grips Dan's hand. "You are not a fool, my friend. A fool is one who knows that he is making a mistake and continues on the same course. All you must do now is change course, and you are wise!"

"Sifu, I *want* to change!" Dan suddenly realizes that his voice has risen several decibels above the level of conversation at the tables around them. He glances hastily around the room, embarrassed, but no one seems to have noticed. He lowers his voice and continues, "But I'm not sure I know *how* to change. Will you teach me?"

Sifu smiles, "Are you asking me to give you assignments?"

Dan reaches into his pocket and pulls out his day planner. "You bet, that'll be great!" he replies enthusiastically. He sits with his pen poised, waiting expectantly.

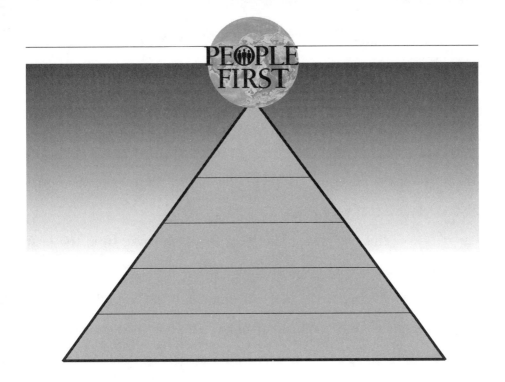

The Pyramid of People Power

*S*ifu beams with pleasure. "Ah, you are a true student! You honor me by writing down my words. Yes, Dan, I will give you suggestions in how to humanize your organization. You may be surprised how easy it is to do, my friend. All it will require is the same kind of consistent effort that you bring to the martial arts.

"Write down these words, Dan: **Truth... Wisdom... Excellence.** You must accept the truth that **people possess exalted dignity, exalted worth, and exalted potentiality.** You must absorb this truth; let it color your every thought, word, and action. Then you must exercise the wisdom to recognize and celebrate the untapped potential in your Purpose Partners. Teach them, tirelessly educate them, about the excellence of their gifts, and work to create a culture that celebrates that excellence.

"Note this, too, Dan: **The best practices come from the best beliefs.** The excellence of your philosophy will be demonstrated by your Purpose Partners. **Do not call your staff 'my people'; instead refer to them as 'my Purpose Partners.'**" Sifu nods towards Dan's day planner, and Dan makes note of the phrase.

Sifu's eyes are very bright. "One of the best ways you can demonstrate those beliefs, Dan, is by using something I call the Pyramid of People Power. If you make these words a part of your daily conversation—all day, every day—and use them with real sincerity and belief, you should see those numbers which have been so troubling, the ones your financial officer provides you, change for the better. May I write in your book?"

"Of course!" Dan quickly slides his day planner across the table to Sifu.

Sifu turns the book so Dan can observe as he writes, then quickly sketches a pyramid. He looks up, his eyes fairly burning into Dan's. "Dan, these are some of the most important words in the English language that a human being can ever hear. They are the words that turn dispirited drones into driven dynamos! They will turn powerless performance puppets into powerful Purpose Partners. Are you ready?"

If anything, Dan's intensity exceeds Sifu's. "Please teach me how to change the way I lead."

"I will teach you how to become a **leader's leader**, Dan, and how to make your company become the purple tile on the grey wall. In other words, you will differentiate yourself from all the spiritually impoverished companies by putting people first. You will become the kind of leader that the room lights up, radiates, and glows... when you walk *into* it." Both men laugh with delight. Sifu resumes his writing, and quickly completes the Pyramid of People Power:

Dan stares down at the paper, then glances quizzically at Sifu. "Sifu, you use these words with us all the time during class!"

Sifu smiles and nods. "Perhaps you thought I was going to give you a complicated formula?

"Dan, has it occurred to you that **every man, woman, and child alive goes through life with the letters MMFI stamped on their foreheads? MMFI stands for Make Me Feel Important.** Every human being *needs* to know that who they are and what they do has meaning and significance. It has been said: 'Only meaning arouses energy.' One of the chief responsibilities of every leader is to communicate as often and as clearly as possible to each one of his Purpose Partners: 'I believe in you; you are significant; your contributions are meaningful and highly valuable.'"

Sifu shakes his head with some distaste. "I meet many business leaders who are far more impressed with themselves than they are with the people they employ. That is not the way of greatness. My Sifu was one of the top champions in China, yet he was perhaps the most humble man I have ever known. The message of his *kwoon* was not 'Sifu first'; we never sensed that he believed, 'I am the Grandmaster, I am the greatest, bow down and worship me.' Rather, his message to us was, 'Every student has exalted worth, exalted dignity, and exalted potential.'"

Sifu smiles warmly at the memory. "He was more impressed with us than he was with himself. He esteemed us more highly than himself. He believed his mission was to bring out the best in us—in *every* aspect of our lives! And he used these words in the Pyramid of People Power every time we were together.

"Think of it this way, Dan; a wise leader will make deposits in the human spirit to keep it in a positive balance, just as he makes deposits in his bank account. In a bank account, the deposits and withdrawals consist of dollars. With people, the deposits consist of the words you use with people, and the care and individual concern you show for them. The withdrawals you make from people's spiritual bank accounts are the things that shut down the human spirit. However, from time to time a leader must correct mistakes, counsel problem Purpose Partners and even occasionally fire recalcitrant ones. But these actions don't have to be perceived as withdrawals if you speak the truth in love. In addition, withdrawals are often made by customers who are rude or impatient. Sometimes they're made by coworkers or even family members who say something unkind. It has been said that it takes ten deposits to make up for one withdrawal."

Sifu is looking intently at Dan, and every trace of humor has vanished from his eyes. "Dan, if you make too many withdrawals from your bank account without making enough deposits, you eventually exhaust all your funds, and the bank will close the account. Similarly, if too many withdrawals are made from a person's spiritual account without any replenishment, that individual's spirit will become exhausted and the account will close down. If the human spirit of your entire staff has shut down, how can your company possibly be competitive, profitable, and customer focused?"

Dan stares at Sifu, shaking his head slowly. "We can't," he says flatly.

"Exactly," Sifu replies. "Dan, many business leaders think their job is all about keeping people working hard in exchange for a paycheck. However, if you utilize this Pyramid of People Power each day, you will be giving out the very *best* kind of paychecks—those which make people rich in their spirit. **Leaders must learn to live in celebration, discovery, and appreciation.** What far too many leaders do not understand is that an attitude of criticism, condemnation, and cynicism throws the kill switch in the human spirit. Instead of turning people on, such communication shuts them down. Some people never recover. Harsh words and a condemning spirit can so injure a sensitive soul that they never regain their self-confidence. This is particularly true of children. A single word can be devastating!"

Sifu's voice takes on an encouraging tone. "We all need good role models if we are to become good leaders. I was very blessed. My Sifu was a giver, a contributor—and not only with his words. He had a big impact on our community. He would take in students who could not afford to attend the *kwoon* and work with them. He did much more than just teach the martial arts; he would sit with these young men and women and discuss qualities such as character, humility, discipline, wisdom, developing a life philosophy, and life strategy for success. The great majority of those young people turned out to be balanced, productive citizens, because **my Sifu cared more about building people than he did about building the bottom line.**"

Sifu pauses for a moment, and a strange, soft look passes across his face. "Dan, I am going to tell you something that not many people know about me: I was one of those students who could not afford my Sifu's school. I wanted more than anything to learn from him, because I had heard he was the finest teacher in China, but my parents were much too poor to pay the required tuition. Somehow he found out about me, and he brought me into the *kwoon* and let me clean the school in payment for the tuition.

"My Sifu put *me* first, Dan. He put my life ahead of his profits. He measured success by the love that his students had for him and for each other, and by the success they had in their lives. He made it possible for me to flourish and grow. And yet, with all the emphasis he placed on people, his *kwoon* was very profitable, because we students told everyone we knew how much we loved our Sifu and his *kwoon*. We loved him because he focused on building our lives and passing on a legacy of truth, wisdom, and excellence to all of us. His *kwoon* was extremely successful, but he was even richer in his spirit. He was a very wealthy man, Dan, in every way you can possibly imagine."

Dan is staring at Sifu in astonishment. "Wow! You've had so much success in your life—you're a world champion, you've got all these students—and you're telling me all this might never have happened?"

Sifu nods. That strange, soft look is now unmistakable. "I was getting deeply involved with a street gang when I was allowed to join the *kwoon*. My whole life changed forever because one man cared enough to invest in me and encourage me to reach for my highest and best. If my Sifu had put profits first, I would never have attended his *kwoon*, and who knows where I would be today? Two of the boys from that gang died in the streets before they turned eighteen."

Dan is deeply impressed. "And if he hadn't done that for you, think of all the people who would never have met you and learned from you." Suddenly another thought occurs to Dan. "And now you're doing that for me, aren't you? You're meeting with me and helping me build my life, and you're not charging me for that. You're putting *me* first."

Sifu's eyes begin to twinkle. "Ah, I simply had not gotten around to asking you to clean the *kwoon* yet!" They both laugh.

Sifu has been watching Dan carefully throughout the conversation, hoping to see signs that his message is getting through. When Dan bursts into laughter, he looks like a man laying down a heavy burden. Dan's body language is changing; his back and shoulders are straight, his eyes are bright, and his voice is growing deeper and more confident. "Sifu, this makes so much sense! You've been telling me that people can't impart what they don't possess. The way I treat my people—" Sifu's lips tighten in mock disapproval and Dan nods and smiles, flushing slightly "—I mean, my Purpose Partners. The way I treat them is what they will turn around and reflect to our customers. If I'm brusque and indifferent with my Purpose Partners, that's what they'll display to our customers. If I value, honor, and respect them, they will value, honor, and respect the customers. If I listen to them, they'll listen to the customers. If I am patient and understanding with them, they'll be gracious with the customers. If I bring out the best in them, they'll give their best to the customers. So I've got to put *people first*! Success starts with them!"

"You are a very good student, Dan," Sifu says, obviously pleased.

PE⊕PLE
FIRST

The
Celebration Exercise

Sifu gives Dan a smile of genuine affection. "I am proud of you, my friend. I have hit you right between the eyes with the flaws in your leadership style. In so many words, I have told you that you don't know that you don't know. Many people would become defensive, even petulant, under such criticism, however well-intentioned. But you have listened, and honestly examined yourself, and freely admitted your failings. That takes real courage and humility. I have high hopes for you and your company!"

Dan looks at Sifu gratefully. "Really? I was just thinking that I'll *never* be able to bring out the best in people like you do."

"Nonsense!" Sifu's voice is brisk, yet kindly. "You have everything it takes to be a world-class leader, Dan." Dan starts to chuckle, but Sifu cuts him off. "I am perfectly serious! **The mind-set precedes the skill sets**, and you are demonstrating that you have the proper mind-set for putting people first. I believe you will succeed in turning your company around."

Dan smiles, and seems to sit a little straighter. "Thank you, Sifu. That means a lot to me."

Sifu beams at Dan. "I am honored that you allow me to encourage you. Now, returning to your workplace; you acknowledge that you and your staff do not live in celebration?"

"No," Dan admits, "we've been living in frustration."

Sifu replies crisply, "Now you will begin turning frustration into celebration. Here is an assignment for you, personally, to carry out, and for you to pass on to every executive, manager, and supervisor in your organization. Every day, Dan, each of you must catch someone doing something *right*... and celebrate it." Sifu raises an admonishing hand. "Do not merely say 'Nice job,' and continue on your way. Stop and talk to the individual, and sincerely praise that person for what he is doing well.

"You see, Dan, many men and women in management have trained themselves to spot what is going wrong, and to correct it. If things are going well, they say nothing; if things are going badly, they spring into action. Now, we have talked about keeping the spiritual bank account full. Every time you or one of your managers points out what one of your Purpose Partners is doing wrong, what happens to that person's account?"

Dan uses his right hand to pantomime the needle of a fuel gauge moving toward empty.

Sifu grins and nods. "Yes, exactly! Your Purpose Partners need fresh deposits put into their accounts on a regular basis in order to maintain a positive balance. So each day, every single person who is in any kind of position of authority must make it a point to catch somebody doing something *right* and celebrate that—they should really make it a point to lift that person's spirits. If you want that positive attitude and action to continue you must recognize it, reinforce it, celebrate it and reward it. Dan, let this transformational model become the joyful role and responsibility of every leader in your company."

Sifu points his index finger at Dan's chest for emphasis. "That takes effort and attention, Dan! Managers simply cannot walk around, saying, 'Nice job, nice job, you are all doing a fine job' to whomever they see. That is a false, meaningless praise, Dan. That kind of flattery can drain the spiritual bank account faster than criticism does, because if you tell somebody that they are doing a 'great job' when they really are *not*, they think, 'If Dan was paying any attention to me, he would know that I am *not* doing a great job! If he cared about me at all, he would understand that I am struggling.'"

Dan nods thoughtfully. "Not only that, but if someone has been performing poorly and one of our managers praises that person, everyone who overhears is negatively affected."

"Precisely right," Sifu says approvingly. "Just remember that this exercise *must* begin with you, Dan. Be on the alert for opportunities to catch those who report to you doing things right, and encourage them to do the same with the men and women who report to them.

"You and your managers recognize what is being done well, so that your praise is sincere and specific. Write these four letters in your notebook, Dan: **S, S, I, P.** They stand for **Sincere, Specific, Immediate, and Personal.** Your celebrations—the praise that you give your Purpose Partners—should always be sincere, specific, immediate, and personal. We have already discussed the first two; when you praise someone, you must first have gone to the trouble of watching what that person is doing, so that you are able to be specific in pointing out what it is that he has done well and sincerely praise him for that particular thing.

"In addition, you and your management team must offer your praise as immediately as possible. I once heard a very wise leader say that **delayed recognition is lost opportunity.** Telling someone that they did a good job on something a week ago is a lost opportunity. Telling someone that they did a good job a month ago is virtually meaningless. You have missed the opportunity to fill up their account while the event is still fresh in their mind."

Sifu is ticking off the points on his fingers as he speaks. "Lastly, make every effort to praise personally. Do not merely say, 'The accounting department did a great job.' Use their names, and point out exactly what each individual did to contribute to the success. Be personal! Yes, it takes extra time and effort to find out what role each individual played, but when you praise them personally, you do so much more to replenish each individual's bank account, and you are much more likely to receive extra effort from them in return.

"And your celebrations will be more effective if you do not send letters or email; go speak to the people personally. Look them in the eye, shake their hand, let them know you value them as a human being. You must consider catching people doing things right and reinforcing that behavior to be one of the most important aspects of your job, Dan. It all begins with you, and you can drive it through the whole organization by the power of your example."

Dan has been busily taking notes. "So, basically, you're saying that I need to take the time to watch what people are doing, so I can see what they're doing well, and then immediately go and tell them personally what they've done well and how much I appreciate their good work. And I have to really mean it!"

Sifu nods, beaming with pleasure. "Yes, very good, my friend! Be sure to encourage everyone on your leadership team to do the same thing. Remember, Dan, your leaders are no different from anyone else on the staff. They cannot impart what they do not possess. So a large portion of your efforts at celebration must be directed at your leaders. You must fill *their* bank account, so that they will be able to go out and make deposits in others. You and your leadership team must become passionate about people! When you learn to speak the language of the human spirit, you will learn how to leverage the power of people and help them maximize their potential."

I AM PROUD OF YOU

"I Am Proud of You!"

$\mathcal{D}$an looked up at Sifu and tapped the pyramid sketched into the day planner before him. "These words you've written here are part of that 'language of the human spirit'?" Sifu nods. "Sifu," Dan says steadily, "You are all about celebrating the human spirit and helping others to reach their fullest potential. I've failed to do that in my company. Will you teach me how to use those words?"

Sifu smiles a broad, reassuring smile. "I will be honored to teach you, Dan." Then the smile disappears, and Sifu is all business. He taps the diagram. "We start at the base of the Pyramid, and here we find **five of the most important words that you can ever say to a human being: 'I am proud of you.'** Dan, do you remember the first time someone said that to you? Was it one of your parents. Perhaps a teacher or a coach?"

Dan's face softens with the recollection. He turns and stares out the window, as if watching the scene being replayed on the street outside. "My junior year of high school, I scored my first touchdown for the varsity football team. It was the game-winner, and my coach grabbed me by the arms, right in front of everybody, and said, 'I am so proud of you!' That was the first time anyone at school ever said something like that to me. I was excited about winning the game, but after he said that..." Dan smiles. "I walked off the field feeling like I was ten feet tall!"

Another thought occurs to Dan, and he swings back to peer at Sifu, something like surprise in his eyes. "Do you know, Sifu, that impacted the way I played for the rest of the year? Football used to be something I did for fun, but I was on a mission after that. I played harder than I ever had, because I wanted to hear the coach say 'I am proud of you' again!" Dan pauses and nods slowly. "I never really thought about it until now, but I got three offers for full football scholarships at Division I schools, and it all goes back to the day my coach said 'I am proud of you.' Those five words really fired up my will to win."

Once again, Dan pauses, looking at Sifu, and his eyes slowly widen. "You've done that for me, ever since I joined your *kwoon*—the night I broke my first board... the night I received the black sash... you've told me so many times that you are proud of me. You do it with all your students. You have a good word for everyone."

Dan looks down at the table for a moment, then directly up at Sifu. "You're saying that if I want to get the best out of the people who work for me, I should do the same thing."

"That is exactly what I am saying." Sifu is suddenly pensive, and he drums his fingers on the table, a gesture unusual in a man who always appears so calm. "Dan, you must not use the things I am teaching you simply to manipulate people's emotions to make them become more productive. This is not just a technique I am teaching you; this is the *right* thing to do, for the right reasons! This is the truth about how everyone should be treated. We should believe the truth and practice the truth.

"You see, Dan, **good words build great people.** I use these words in the Pyramid because they make the people around me more powerful. I want these words to permeate the *kwoon*, and they should permeate your company, as well. How many business leaders have you met, Dan, who were more interested in holding on to their personal power and the power of their position, than they cared about building up the people around them? They withheld power, they didn't give it away. Dan, that which you withhold diminishes, but that which you give away is multiplied. I have met a great many people like that.

"Write this down, Dan: **True power is the power that makes other people powerful.** I make people powerful by teaching them the discipline of the martial arts. You can make people powerful, Dan, by the power you invest in them through your words. When a true leader observes anybody in their charge exhibiting positive change of any kind, that leader will say so—not merely observe the change. Let your focus be on your Purpose Partners, Dan, not yourself. Let people see and hear that you value them more highly than you value yourself. Put people first."

Dan's jaw sets. "Sifu, I just never saw it that way. I'm going to start doing things a *lot* differently at the office."

Sifu's voice is very soft. "Not just at the office, Dan. There is someplace even more important." Sifu is looking deep into Dan's eyes, and Dan suddenly realizes what is coming. He drops his eyes to the table, wincing slightly. "Dan, when was the last time you told your wife, 'I am proud of you?' When have you used these words with your children?"

Dan shakes his head guiltily. It has been so long that he cannot remember. "Sifu, I'm just not good at doing that. I guess I'm more of a high-tech person; I'm just not a high-touch guy."

Sifu dismisses the statement with a shake of his head. "Dan, as important as it is for you to use these words at your company, it is *far* more important for you to use them with your family. Take this philosophy of high discovery and high development into your home. Delight in your wife! Discover who she is, and tell her how much you love what you find. Discover who your children are, and praise them. Help them develop their God-given talents, and delight in their accomplishments *and* their efforts! You told me a moment ago how much it meant to you when your coach praised you. How much more important for your children to hear those words from *you*, Dan."

Sifu pauses for a moment, then raps his knuckles briskly on the table, like a judge calling for order in the courtroom. "Dan, let me issue you a challenge. These timeless truths we have been discussing must begin in your home. I want you to go to your wife, look her in the eye, and ask her this question: 'How do you feel about yourself when you are around me?' If she says nothing—perhaps you see a little tick in her cheek, and her eyes look like those of a deer frozen in the headlights of your car, she has answered you as clearly as if she had spoken. You may safely assume that she is thinking, *'I dislike myself the most when I am around you.'*" Sifu looks steadily at Dan. "Dan, do you expect that she might answer that way?"

Dan looks back at Sifu. His mouth moves, but no words come. Then he drops his eyes.

Sifu speaks slowly, gently: "The assignment should help you see how 'high-tech without high-touch,' as you say, drains the spiritual bank account in your home. Dan, I heard an expression several years ago: 'You have fame with the world, but no name with your family.' This will always be true, until you begin to practice the People First philosophy with your wife and children. Now, Cheryl is an adult, and she is responsible for keeping herself renewed spiritually, but as her husband, it is your responsibility to make frequent deposits in her spiritual account. You must do your part to keep your marriage strong by letting her know how much you value her."

Sifu pauses for a moment, then smiles and says, "Tell me some of the things that Cheryl does which would cause you to sincerely say, 'I am proud of you.'"

Dan needs to think for only a moment. "Well, there are a lot of things I could tell you. She's a wonderful mother to our children—patient and loving and fair. You couldn't ask for a better model as a mother. I'm also proud of her for how she performs at her job. A couple of top executives have told me that she's the best meeting planner they know." Dan is warming to the subject. "On top of all that, she keeps a beautiful home... and she's a *great* hostess; people love to visit with us."

Sifu nods. "So there are several things Cheryl does that you are proud of! When was the last time you talked to her about these things, and told her that you are proud of her?"

Dan's mouth shuts with a snap that is practically audible. He stares wordlessly at Sifu.

Sifu smiles a sad smile. "You have *thought* about these things, have you not?"

"Oh, yes, I *think* about them, but I've never... really... told her."

Dan's voice trails off, and he is speaking more to himself than to the man across the table. "Lately, we haven't really talked about much of anything..." Dan looks defensively at Sifu. "Sifu, I wasn't raised in a family where people said these things."

"All the more reason for you to break the cycle of silence in your home... and in your business," Sifu replies evenly. "Dan, you must remember this: **The personal drives the professional.** The way you behave in your personal life will be revealed in your professional life; your professional philosophy flows out of your personal philosophy. A man cannot live in celebration at work and in criticism at home. You must put people first *all* the time; do not treat this philosophy like a lab coat that you put on when you arrive at the office and leave on a hangar when you go home. Dan, since I have been talking to you this morning, I have not been functioning in some artificial role as the Grandmaster. I have been real with you. I live the People First philosophy where ever I am or whatever I am doing. I think too many people hide behind their titles and they are not real. This is called an integrity gap. There is a disconnect between who they are and what they display to the world. Dan, people follow authenticity and not hypocrisy. Now Dan, I encourage you to practice the people first philosophy at home first.

"Dan, how do you think Cheryl would feel if you told her that you are proud of her—that you really appreciate her?"

"I think she'd suspect I'd been drinking!" Dan replies wryly, and they both laugh.

"Dan, as I said before, people—your wife and children, espe-cially—need to know that who they are and what they do has meaning and significance. Your family will never know what you are thinking until you express it! It is very good that you have all those positive thoughts about Cheryl. You *do* take notice of all she does. But what good does it do *her* that you hold these positive thoughts about her if she never receives them?

Dan nods unhappily. "It doesn't do her any good at all. But Sifu," Dan objects dolefully. "I've been this way all my life. I've always been functional and not personal. Do you *really* think I can change?"

Sifu looks steadily at Dan. "The real question is, do you *want* to change?"

"I *do* want to change, Sifu! I don't want things to keep going in the same direction..." Suddenly, without warning, Dan's eyes begin to fill and a tear runs down his cheek. Sifu quickly busies himself stirring his coffee, but Dan struggles to speak again.

"Sifu, I'm sorry, it's just that talking about this reminded me of how much I always wanted my dad to say that... *he* was proud of me." Dan's voice is broken and rough. "My mother used to say it, but my dad *never* said he was proud of me. I used to ask my mother, 'What's *wrong* with me? Why is it that dad never says he's proud of me?'

My mother would say, 'Dan, it's hard for him to say those things. He *is* proud of you; he has told me so, but his father never spoke that way to him, and I just don't think your father knows how to talk that way'... And I don't Sifu..." More tears start to stream down Dan's cheeks.

Sifu reaches across the table, and grips Dan's forearm. "It is painful to speak of these things, my friend. But sometimes it is even more painful to keep them locked up inside."

Dan brushes roughly, almost angrily, at the tears on his face. This was *not* what he expected to be discussing this morning! "Sifu, I don't want it to be like that for my kids... I *swore* to myself that I'd be different from my father... dad died when he was fifty-four years old. Six months before he died, he finally said it: 'Son, I'm so proud of you. I should have told you years ago.' We hugged... and we both cried..." Once again, Dan's voice breaks and he stops speaking. Sifu waits quietly for Dan to compose himself.

Dan pushes out a shaky laugh, looking around the room and wiping his eyes with his handkerchief. "I don't imagine many executives come in here and start crying all over the table," he whispers to Sifu.

"You might be surprised, Dan," Sifu smiles. "I am quite sure there are a great many who would like to."

Dan smiles back, and his voice is steadier, but still very soft: "I never did understand why it took dad so long to say that to me. Do you know what else he said? 'Don't be like me,' he said. 'Don't raise your children the way I raised you.' I told him I wouldn't—and Sifu, I am raising my children *exactly* the same way my dad raised me! What you said before about how important it is for my kids to hear me say 'I'm proud of you...' You'd think if anybody understood that, it would be me!" He looks at Sifu and shakes his head, genuinely bewildered. "And here I am doing the same thing! You spoke of a 'cycle of silence.' My word! That's exactly what it is! I've got to change, Sifu. I've *got* to!"

Sifu leans across the table toward Dan, and his voice is strong and confident. "Dan, you have already made the most important step toward lasting change; you have become willing! The Chinese say that a journey of one thousand miles begins with one step. You can take the first step today by telling Cheryl how proud you are of her. And tell your children. Show them your human side, Dan. Let them see your humanity, just as you have with me this morning. Dan, the greatest leaders are the ones that are the most human. You are not weak because you have shed tears in a public place. You have honored me, Dan, by showing me your heart and being transparent and vulnerable. We bond with and trust leaders that are genuine and that are willing to reveal their imperfections."

Dan smiles weakly, "Well, I feel like a big baby, crying like this."

"Not at all, my friend," Sifu assures him kindly, waving a dismissive hand. "You should not be ashamed. Emotion is a vital part of being human. It is an act of love and trust to open one's heart so freely and so fully. I am humbled by this. Dan, never forget this, people do not put walls around strength, but weakness. You are displaying your strength by bearing your soul to me. And you will honor your family in the same way by the disclosure and openness with which you reveal yourself. Dan, you are becoming an authentic person, and it is beautiful to behold."

Dan's voice is stronger and his eyes are clearing. "Sifu, what you're really talking about is me reinventing me, aren't you?"

Sifu chuckles. "This word you use—'reinventing'—it is a word we hear politicians use a great deal lately. But the leopard does not very often change his spots! No, Dan, I am talking about being totally human and alive totally. I am talking about recognizing that which has always been within you—the need for meaning and significance—and acknowledging that every man, woman, and child you meet has that same need! I am talking about contribution, Dan, about giving power away in order to make other people powerful. Instead of using a word like 'reinventing,' think in terms of 'reawakening.'"

Dan has been scribbling hastily on his pad. "And this reawakening should start in my home. I begin at home and then take it to the office. I use the words in the Pyramid of People Power in order to practice living in celebration, discovery, and appreciation."

Sifu smiles and nods. "You are a very good student, Dan. **Become the official 'right-finder' in your home and in your office— not the official fault-finder.** Once again, let me caution you that this is not for manipulation; putting people first is about ministry, not manipulation. You are to minister selflessly to their spirit, not manipulate their emotions."

Dan takes some more notes. Reading upside-down as best he can, Sifu watches Dan write; "Live in celebration and discovery with Cheryl, the kids, and the staff. *Purpose Partners!* Be the official right-finder. Minister to the human spirit." Dan looks up at Sifu, and is rewarded with one of Sifu's brightest smiles. "I'd like to be a fly on the wall at your home and office during the next few weeks," Sifu says warmly.

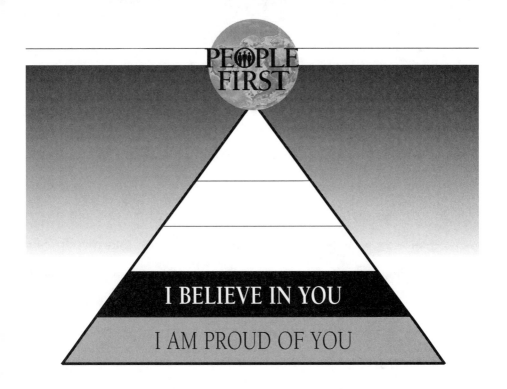

I BELIEVE IN YOU

I AM PROUD OF YOU

"I Believe in You!"

"Tell me more, Sifu," Dan says eagerly. "I want to learn all of this. You tell us to come to your *kwoon* with an empty cup—to be teachable. Well, here I am, as empty a cup as you'll ever find; fill me up!"

Sifu throws back his head and laughs delightedly. "Very well, my friend, let us discuss four of the most important words in the English language: '**I believe in you.**' Dan, here are words to write down and remember: **The exclamation point behind success is belief.** You *must* believe in your Purpose Partners if they are to believe in themselves. On the night you were preparing to break a brick with a palm strike for the first time, I said, 'I believe in you.' And you replied, 'I'm not sure I believe in myself.' Do you remember what I told you?"

Dan smiles. "You said, 'Borrow my faith in you until you have developed your own.' I remember looking into your eyes, and it was written all over your face that you believed in me. I told myself: *'Sifu has taught thousands of people, and he knows what a person is capable of doing. He's observed me for five years; if he believes I can break this brick, I must be able to break it!'* So I did exactly what you said; I borrowed your faith! I set myself, and I didn't even think about the brick, I just screamed and hit right through it. That was such an awesome moment! And you're absolutely right; if I hadn't been so sure you believed I could do it, I might not even have tried."

Dan has been speaking animatedly, but suddenly his hands drop to his sides and his face falls. "Sifu, I haven't done that at all for other people. I haven't been believing in my family or my peop—I mean, my Purpose Partners at work." Dan frowns. "That's *especially* true at work. In fact, I usually expect them to do poor work." Dan looks at Sifu, his eyes widening. "Sifu, I've been *preparing* my staff to fail, haven't I?!"

Sifu nods sadly. "A man's family and his company are simply the out-living of his in-living beliefs. They reflect his beliefs in them and about them. **Belief is the center and circumference of human achievement.** If the belief is not there to under gird every step, there will be no advancement in any aspect of a person's life."

Sifu looks meaningfully at Dan. Dan understands that something important is coming and prepares to write another note. **"I do not believe in the saying, 'Seeing is believing.' I believe in its opposite: Believing is seeing.** Write that down, Dan: 'Believing is seeing.' You hear people who are poor in their spirit say, 'I will believe it when I see it.' Dan, if I had waited until I saw you do things—if my faith in you was dependent on seeing all that you could do before I *believed* in all that you could do—you would not have achieved as you have. If I operated under the philosophy of 'Seeing is believing' the night you stood poised to break that first brick, you would have looked at my face and seen nothing but a blank stare, because I had not seen you break a brick yet! It is likely that the doubt in my eyes would have created fear in your own heart, and you might well have failed. But when you looked into my face, there was not a glimmer of doubt, only tremendous confidence, because my face is a mirror of my belief."

Sifu's eyes are riveted on Dan's. It is as if he is trying to transfer the very essence of his being into Dan just by the force of his concentration. Dan has seen the same intensity on Sifu's face when he has competed in international matches. "Dan, where there is fear, there is no faith! The two are mutually exclusive. In all of my years of competition, I have fought hundreds of competitors—many of them very talented men. I have watched some of these men lose their belief right in front of me, right there in the ring! Their body language tells me they no longer have faith in their ability to win. In that moment, Dan, when they *believed* that they could not succeed, they lost the match. Oh, it may take another minute for that unbelief to become reality, but the outcome is certain. As soon as I see them lose faith in themselves, I move in to win the match, because I know their faith has been replaced by fear.

"I have learned a great many lessons about business in the arena, Dan. A competitor may not be as skilled or powerful as his more gifted opponent, but if he enters the match with an undaunted, unassailable, unconquerable faith, that belief will often enable him to succeed.

"I operate under the philosophy of 'Believing is seeing,' because *that mind-set reflects reality*, Dan! A farmer goes out and sows a handful of seeds; he believes God will bring the rain and sunshine so the crop will grow before it ever happens. Some leaders pride themselves on being able to see the seed in the apple, but **a truly great leader is one who sees the apple inside the seed.** That is the essence of 'Believing is seeing.'

"You must believe that your Purpose Partners will excel, Dan, and communicate that belief. *Then* the corporate trainers you hire to work with the staff will provide the skill sets to express the mind-set of excellence. Belief is the basis for behavior. If you supply the belief, Dan, your Purpose Partners will respond with the kind of customer-first behavior you desire."

Sifu taps his index finger on the table to add emphasis to his words. "Dan, every *moment* that you interact with your Purpose

Partners, they *know* whether or not you believe in them. Your body language, the tone of your voice, the *words* you use—all work together to *constantly* communicate your belief in them... or your disbelief. My Sifu's body, his voice, and his words *shouted* to us how much he believed in us! There was strong congruence in his communication; his body language and the tone of his voice communicated, 'I believe in you,' just as clearly as the actual words he used. We drank in that positive communication, Dan, like plants drink in water, and we became powerful manifestations of his belief in us. Dan, because of his belief in the incalculable worth of the human spirit, he was committed to unlocking the treasure talent chest within every person he met. By his example, he taught us to treasure each other."

Dan shakes his head slowly. "I've got *so* much work to do," he admits sheepishly. "You're telling me that my company is going to reflect my belief, but I don't believe in the people! And because I've been expecting failure, our company is fearful; we're not faith-full."

Sifu wags an admonishing finger at Dan. "Begin speaking in the past tense: 'Our company was fearful.' Here is a proverb for you to remember and use, Dan: 'Fear knocked at the door, but faith answered it, and there was no one there.'"

Dan is silent for a moment, writing carefully. Then he raises his head, and Sifu is pleased to see a new light of understanding there, and yes—at last there is hope. "You're telling me I must have that faith— that belief—within myself, and I must communicate that faith to my

Purpose Partners at every turn. I've got to 'lend them my faith.'"

"Yes, Dan, that is very good!" Sifu says warmly, "Give them your belief. Tell them that you see the apple inside of the seed. Tell them every day! Dan, there are many things that can create fear within an organization. Companies are dealing with change, responding to competition, reacting to the unexpected... all these factors can hinder a company's performance. Your Purpose Partners need to draw closer together to be unified—*especially* during difficult times—and believe in each other, their principles, their products, and their services. *That* is how a company will successfully navigate through change and turbulent times."

Once again, Sifu motions toward Dan's day planner. "I once read **a great acronym for FAITH: Fearless Attitudes Inspiring Troubled Hearts.** Dan, you must rally everyone in your company around your belief in People First. Let them know—first, foremost, and always—that you believe in them. Inspire their hearts with your faith.

"I read books on business management, as I know you do, Dan. Virtually all of the books that are big sellers employ the same term: they speak of the 'best business practices.' The writers claim to have initiated the 'best practices' in their field, but what they fail to address is even more fundamental. They must first adopt the best beliefs! The best beliefs are the basis for the best practices; the best philosophy is *foundational* to peak performance. It has been well said that the incorporation of sound furnishings does not make up for an unsound foundation. **Sow your seeds of belief liberally throughout your company,**

Dan and you will reap a great harvest of happy Purpose Partners, happy customers, happy shareholders, and long-term profits."

Dan is writing furiously in his day planner, pausing to glance up at Sifu. The light of new hope is burning bright in his eyes. "Sifu, this is great stuff! I can't *wait* to put it all into practice."

At that moment, the waitress approaches, and Dan leans across the table and whispers to Sifu, "Tell me her name again?"

Sifu murmurs the name to him, and Dan leans back and looks directly up at the waitress when she asks if the two men would like anything else. "Cynthia," he says. "We'd like some more coffee, but I have to tell you something first." Cynthia looks warily down at Dan, obviously expecting to field a complaint. Her cautious demeanor melts when Dan says, "I just want you to know that I'm proud of you. You've been waiting on us all this time, even though we've been sitting here talking for quite awhile now, and you've been very gracious and effi-cient. You are very good at your job, and you're a credit to your employer. I just wanted to say 'Thank you,' and to tell you that I plan to leave you an extra good tip."

Cynthia's face lights up with genuine pleasure. "Thank you, sir. You have no idea how nice it is to hear you say that! Two of my cus-tomers were *very* rude this morning, and I was feeling kinda low. You just wiped all that away. Thanks!" She walks away from the table smiling happily, and even a casual observer would see a new spring in her step."

Sifu's smile extends from ear to ear. "Dan, you did not wait to get to work or go home to start using the Pyramid, you wanted to start right now!"

Dan chuckles delightedly. "I can't believe I'm doing this! It's like trying on a 'new me'! It feels a little awkward, but you know what? I like it! And you're right, Sifu, it all started with me and my attitude toward her. When I was personal and human with her, it made all the difference in the world. I felt better, and she felt better, you could see it as plain as day. This philosophy of yours really works!"

Dan grins at his teacher. "I believe in *you*, Sifu. This is the best business seminar I've ever been to in my life—sitting in a restaurant drinking coffee! You've given me hope that I can change, and that I can become a change agent for others. Teach me more! The next words you've written in the Pyramid are: 'I need you.' I can't wait to hear what you have to say on *this* one." Dan rubs his hands together briskly, like a man sitting down to a good meal.

Suddenly, Sifu's face changes dramatically; it becomes cold and inscrutable. "You come clean *kwoon* first," he commands in harsh, pidgin English. "Then Sifu teach next three words." Dan freezes for an instant, startled by the radical change in Sifu's speech and demeanor. Then he spies that familiar twinkle in the Grandmaster's eyes, and he realizes that Sifu is teasing him. Dan bursts into laughter, and Sifu joins him. This time, Dan doesn't even notice when a few heads in the restaurant turn at the sound of their full-throated merriment.

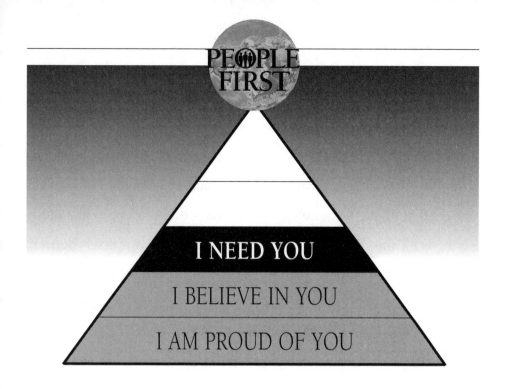

I NEED YOU

I BELIEVE IN YOU

I AM PROUD OF YOU

"I Need You!"

$\mathcal{S}$ifu pauses to wipe tears of mirth from his eyes. "Dan," he says, still chuckling. "What would happen if you arrived at work one morning and told all your Purpose Partners to go home, because you were going to operate the company all by yourself?"

"Nothing would get done," Dan promptly replies. "It isn't a one-man organization. It takes a team of talented individuals to be successful."

"Precisely right," Sifu nods. "If you have staffed well, each individual's contribution is vital to the success of the organization. But Dan, how many leaders convey the message to their Purpose Partners—the most invaluable of all assets—which is perceived as: 'You are expendable; I really do not need you in order to succeed'?"

Dan nods, beginning to feel uncomfortable again. What Sifu is saying is all too true; Dan has met many men and women who treat staffers that way. Dan is becoming increasingly certain that he, himself, has behaved in the very way Sifu is describing. Sure enough, Sifu's next question cuts right to the heart of the matter.

"Let us take you and your wife as an example. Do you need her?"

"Yes, I need her!" Dan is emphatic.

"Why do you need her?"

Dan hesitates for only a moment as he collects his thoughts, wanting to be completely honest with his teacher. "I need her companionship, I need her love, I need her support... I need her to be there for me."

Sifu nods and smiles. "Dan, I can hear by the tone of your voice that you are very sincere." He pauses for a moment, and Dan's stomach knots as he anticipates Sifu's next question.

"Has Cheryl heard you say these words? With that same conviction in your voice?"

Dan sighs. "Sifu, this is another major area I need to work on. Without Cheryl, there would be no family. I couldn't have raised our children without her. I'm hardly ever home! And I know I wouldn't be the person I am without Cheryl. She always believed in me, even during the times when I didn't believe in myself. She encourages me... she really is the wind beneath my wings."

Dan scowls and shakes his head. "I haven't told her *any* of those things. I'm sure I act like I don't really need her, and I *know* that's how I behave toward the people who work for me. I've worked very hard to build that company, but I've given myself far too much credit for the success we've enjoyed in years past. The question you asked a moment ago about sending everybody home really pinpoints the issue: without the people in the company, there would be no company." Dan's eyes widen. "That's why you're telling me to call them 'Purpose Partners'! *They* interact with the customers, not me. They're the image-bearers of the organization—not me. I've been acting—and thinking—like it's all about me."

Dan shakes his head again, grimacing. He is angry with himself, but when he speaks, his voice is plaintive. "Sifu, what else can I do to bring this philosophy to life in my company?"

"Dan, you must realize that the human spirit is larger than any job you can put it in. You must **broaden the borders of the job with meaning.** These words, 'I need you,' speak to the importance of meaning."

Sifu smiles. "Think of it this way, Dan. What was the very first word your children started to speak—after they learned 'No'?"

Dan chuckles, then thinks for a moment. "Well, I don't know if it was the first word, but the word they kept on saying, over and over, was 'Why?'"

"Yes, that very word!" Sifu says delightedly. "Children are eternal question-boxes, always asking, 'Why, Mommy?' 'Why, Daddy?'"

"About 50,000 times a day," Dan agrees wearily.

Sifu is completely animated. "The need for meaning and purpose is so strong within the human spirit, Dan! We all want to know 'why.' And the vast majority of us do not become any less curious as we grow older; we just become more sophisticated at masking our curiosity. If someone gives us a new job to do, we want to know why. If there is a change in policy, we want to know why. If staffers are hired or fired or laid off, we want to know why.

The worst thing you can hear staffers say, my friend, is... Sifu gives a very passable imitation of a typical employee. "'Don't ask *me*, I just *work* here.' Staffers must feel connected to the organization by meaning. If they do not, it is virtually impossible for them to perform with passion. Remember what I told you before that: 'Only meaning arouses energy.' Purpose gives birth to passion.

"Dan, people will tend to live up to your expectations if you clearly communicate what those expectations are. If you want your Purpose Partners to operate at maximum effectiveness, you must not allow them to view their jobs in isolation; they must understand how they contribute to the big picture. There should be no 'little people' and no 'little places' in your company. Show each individual how his or her job contributes to the success of the organization. Give *meaning* to what they do! The operative word is *connection.*"

Sifu raps on the table for emphasis. "The job of the leader is to connect the individual with the overall purpose of the organization. The whole gives meaning to the parts, Dan. Once an individual sees and understands the whole, and how their part contributes to the success of the whole, *then* they will realize how much you need them. Then you are not telling them, 'I need you to work from nine-to-five turning out widgets,' but rather you are saying 'I *need* you, because without your meaningful contribution, our overall purpose will suffer.'

"Every human being needs to know that they are needed... that who they are and what they do in a company—or in a family—has purpose, meaning, and immense significance. It is this sense of interconnection that makes the difference between an organization that is powerful and profitable and one that is unanchored and ineffectual.

"When you go home and speak to Cheryl, Dan, and tell her, 'I am proud of you; I believe in you; I need you; I could not do any of this without you.' Remember what we said about SSIP. Be sincere when you speak to her; be specific in telling her what she does that is so important to you. Do it immediately. And, make your communication with her personal... *meaningful!*"

Sifu pauses for a moment, and smiles softly, almost shyly, at Dan. "I need you, Dan."

Dan is startled. "*You* need *me*, Sifu? You're a Walu Grandmaster; an international world champion! If I left your school today, you'd still have thousands of other students. You're a success in every way I can see. How could you possibly need me?"

Sifu gently replies, "Dan, we have been discussing the importance of putting people before profits. Let us dig deeper, down to the bedrock of this philosophy. Remember, what I said earlier, that when the student is ready the teacher will appear. However, it is also true that when the teacher is ready, the student will appear. They really need each other, and this gives meaning to the relationship. Therefore, organizations must be *meaning*-driven before they are profit-driven. Your growth, Dan—your progress in the martial arts and maturation as a man—provides me with meaning. My work provides me with a true sense of significance when my students excel. So I need you, Dan, to tap your potential if I am going to see my work as having meaning! When you look at work in that light, we all need each other to tap our potential. We need to connect with each other, to believe in one another, to support each other, and encourage each other. We need each other to grow, if we ourselves are going to grow. Dan, I believe some people think that if they honor other people it will take away from them. However, when we celebrate and honor others for who they are, we actually create an environment that blends our persons to create beautiful music together. It is like a talented orchestra playing all their instruments in harmony. If each member of the orchestra didn't highly honor the individual talents of their fellow team members, and respectfully blend their instruments with the others, there would be cacophony and not symphony. They need to connect to each other to beautify the world."

Dan is staring at Sifu through narrowed eyes, and he is hanging on Sifu's every word. "Sifu," Dan says slowly. "You're so *right*! But I had never thought about these things."

Sifu gives Dan an encouraging smile. "Many men and women live an entire lifetime and never come to this realization. True growth, Dan, occurs as we grow in our relationships. During our conversation this morning, you and I have grown in our relationship, have we not? We have built bridges of trust and connection with each other. *I need you*, Dan, in order to grow! I need to impart what I have learned, and I need your support and encouragement. I also need to listen to your questions and objections, your comments and your criticism—everything you say, because that sharpens and refines my own thinking. Another proverb, Dan, that we often hear is, 'As iron sharpens iron, so one man sharpens another.' You and I need each other if we are to be sharp and strong."

Dan has been sitting motionless, the pen in his hand completely forgotten. "Sifu, this goes much deeper than I'd ever realized. I never saw my team members as being necessary for my personal growth."

Dan flushes slightly. "To be honest," he admits. "I saw them as a vehicle for my own professional success. If they performed well, I'd do well." Dan shakes his head wonderingly. "But you're telling me that I need other people to succeed in order to reach *my* fullest potential for success!"

Sifu nods, smiling. "That's right, Dan, we all need each other if we are to grow strong as individuals. It has been well said that 'No man is an island.'" Sifu's face hardens. "The curse that will bring down any man or woman is becoming self-occupied, self-serving, and self-seeking. This mind-set is poisonous to the philosophy of People First and the sincere belief that 'I need you.' Another proverb, Dan, for every leader to remember is this: 'Humility goes before honor.' The person who walks in humility says, 'I need you'; the prideful person says, 'I need no one.' You must never let yourself become a prisoner of your own self-importance."

Dan is visibly abashed. "Sifu, here's another rung on this Pyramid of People Power where you've put me in front of a mirror and shown me that there are huge warts all over my face! I've always prided myself on being 'independent.' It never even occurred to me that I was simply being prideful! 'I need you' means that I need people. I *really* need my wife... and my kids! They're in my life to help me grow, and I'm in their lives for their growth. Sifu, I haven't exercised *any* of these principles in my home, where they should have been applied first, foremost, and always. I've got to tell you that it's painful to look at all these things and see what a lousy leader I've been in my home... *and* in my business!"

Sifu makes a slashing gesture with his right hand, cutting off Dan's words. "We are to learn from our failures Dan. A 'lousy leader' is one who looks in the mirror and walks away, and immediately forgets what he looks like and is not educated by his failures. You are looking in the mirror for the first time, and you are determined to learn and make changes. That makes you a great leader, a wise man, and a loving husband and father. Change is a matter of dying to your old self, and that takes time. But there is a new self that is coming to life with this new philosophy, and that should be exciting, not painful."

Dan brightens at Sifu's words. "Well, I'm glad I came face-to-face with this now, rather than going through my whole life without understanding it." There is no more doubt in Dan's eyes—only determination. "Sifu, I can see that you are sharing real wisdom with me. This philosophy is exactly what I need."

Again, Sifu nods in recognition of Dan's praise. "Dan, I have tried to live my life according to the words my Sifu repeated to us again and again: 'Wisdom is the principal thing; therefore get wisdom.' I have sought out people of wisdom, so that I could listen and learn from them. We need a great deal more wisdom in the world of business. Many business leaders seem to believe that profits are the principal thing, not wisdom.

"Dan, as a business leader you must think wise thoughts. Never forget this proverb Dan, '**As a man thinks in his heart so is he.**' That is the most profound definition of a person I have ever learned. **A person is what they think.** Dan, I am listening to the thoughts of your mind and you are becoming a different person before my eyes. You are believing and thinking the wise thoughts of the Pyramid of People Power. I need you to continue on this path of becoming a wise leader."

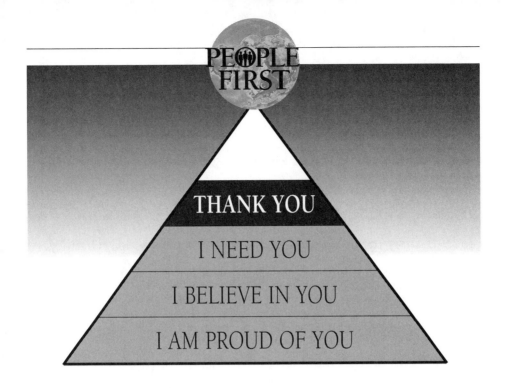

PEOPLE FIRST

THANK YOU

I NEED YOU

I BELIEVE IN YOU

I AM PROUD OF YOU

"Thank You!"

*L*et us move toward the top of the Pyramid, Dan, and look at the wise application of two of the most important words a human being can hear, which are '**Thank you**.' Dan, when we end our classes at the *kwoon*, the students line up and face the teacher, and we salute each other.

"And you say, 'Shay-shay'—'Thank you' in Chinese." Dan says, paying close attention. "Then the students say, 'Shay-shay, Sifu,' meaning 'Thank you, Sifu.'"

Sifu nods. "That tradition has been maintained for more than five hundred years in our schools. Notice who initiates the giving of thanks. It is the teacher who first thanks the students. He is thanking them for their hard work, for respecting each other, and respecting the art. The teacher sets the example by showing his appreciation for the students first, then the students reciprocate by saying, 'Thank you, Sifu.' They are thanking the teacher for sharing his knowledge with patience and humility.

"One of the greatest lessons that anyone can learn, Dan, is not only to live in the understanding of who people are, but also to live in appreciation. We let others know that we appreciate them by saying, 'Thank you.'

"My Sifu gave our *kwoon* a tremendous lesson in appreciation. One evening, the circus had come to town, and he took us all to see it. We sat there in awe, watching people who demonstrated some of the best balance, agility, and poise that we had ever seen. We could recognize the greatness of their ability, and our own training had taught us to appreciate how hard those performers had practiced in order to make something so difficult look effortless.

"When the performance was over, we all expected to leave, but our Sifu had a surprise for us. He knew a few of the circus performers personally, and he had been able to obtain a backstage pass for our group. We watched our teacher, who was the top Grandmaster in China and a star in his own right, as he introduced himself to the various performers. He told them all, with such great sincerity, 'Thank you for a magnificent performance. My students and I have been so honored to witness these incredible feats.'

"I had never seen anyone do such a thing: to watch a performance and then go to the performers and say 'Thank you.' You could see that these men and women really delighted in the genuine appreciation he expressed to them. And when they heard our Grandmaster's name and realized who he was, they were deeply honored that he attended to them that way. Many of them had seen his matches; and yet here was the champion of China coming to them and telling them he had been delighted to watch them. It made a great impact on me, Dan, seeing how humble he was, and how those circus performers drew strength from his words.

"Back at our *kwoon*, our Sifu talked to us several times during the weeks that followed about the importance of living in appreciation. He told us that, while we were at our high schools and colleges, we should watch for those occasions when one of our teachers or professors did a truly great job of imparting wisdom to the students—really poured themselves into their students and gave of themselves completely. Yet, he said, normally what happens when the class ends, the students file out, and no one offers a word of thanks to the teacher. These men and women have dedicated their lives to teaching young people... yet they received virtually no appreciation for their efforts. My Sifu challenged everyone in our *kwoon* to make a conscious effort to sincerely thank our teachers and praise them for all the work they put into preparing for our classes.

"Our Sifu told us to expand this thinking to every area of our lives where people serve us. He asked us how many of us had ever said 'Thank you' to the garbage man, or our mail carrier, or a policeman. Of course, none of us had. He told us that he believed that saying 'Thank you' actually beautified the environment. Dan, I watched that man over the years, and I saw how people would light up and become more purposeful and more powerful after their interaction with him, and I came to believe that he was right. His sincere words of thanks beautified the culture. And I realized that he was challenging us to take one of the most important steps a man or woman can take for personal growth and maturity—the step of putting people first." Sifu gives Dan a searching look, hoping to see that Dan is absorbing the message. "I look for opportunities every day to demonstrate appreciation for my teachers, and especially for those who serve me.

"There was something else my Sifu had to say about this subject: **One's character is revealed by how he treats the people who serve him.** He explained that, in reality, we are all in the role of master and servant to each other. For example, Dan, I am your Walu Kung Fu Grandmaster; but as your teacher I am also your servant. Here at this restaurant, we call Cynthia our 'server.' Yet she is also our master in this setting. She is in complete control of whether our meal arrives steaming hot or only lukewarm. If we are unpleasant to her, we may find ourselves waiting a very long time for our food!"

Sifu pauses, and Dan feels his stomach tighten as he anticipates what Sifu is likely to say next: *"How is it in your company, Dan? What do you reveal about your character in the way you treat those who work for you? Do you see the importance of telling those who serve at your company, 'Thank you?'"* Instead, Sifu smiles and asks, "Have you ever had someone give you a card or a thank you note for something you did?"

Dan's face brightens. "My first job after college was for a man who used to write little notes and attach them to our paychecks. It was no big deal, really, just a sentence or two. One time he wrote, 'I am so blessed and grateful that you came to work here.' It was just a few words, but it meant so much to me... I saved some of those notes for years." Dan's lips tighten. "I don't know why I never thought of doing that for anyone else."

There is not even a hint of criticism in Sifu's voice. "Well, you have thought of it now. Dan, who are the unsung heroes in your company? Who has a 'thankless' job?"

Dan takes a moment to consider, his brows knitted together in a frown of concentration. "Well, one area would be our switchboard operators. We *expect* phone calls to be answered quickly and courteously. We *expect* that callers won't get stuck on hold or disconnected. That's the job. So usually the only time one of our operators hears from a supervisor is when something has gone wrong."

Dan pauses again and nods in dawning understanding. "Now

that you mention it, Sifu, there are a *lot* of positions like that. Our janitors, for example. We *expect* the place to be clean; generally the only interaction we'll have with janitors is to tell them when we've found a mess they haven't cleaned up yet. And we expect our accounting department to get checks out on time and in the right amount. We might go years without commenting on their work—until a check doesn't get sent, or there's some kind of foul-up. Then we suddenly have a *lot* to say about their work! That's also true for our cashiers and front-line personnel. The only time anybody notices them is when they make a mistake or someone complains."

Sifu prods gently, "So these people may not believe that you appreciate them?"

Dan's angry response is directed at himself, not Sifu. "How *could* they feel appreciated? The only time they hear from me is when I'm unhappy about something!" Dan pauses for a moment, and lowers his voice. "Just the other day, I barked at my secretary because she forgot to give me a message. Sifu, that woman makes a mistake about once every six months. She's there every day, never misses a day, and she's everything you could ask for: polite, cheerful, and highly efficient. But I don't compliment her for the hundreds of things she gets right; instead, I blasted her for the one thing she did wrong."

Dan heaves a deep sigh and turns to stare out the window. Then he turns back to Sifu, and there is a steely glint of determination in his eyes. "If I run my company the way you run your kwoon, my whole company might be transformed."

"*Will* be transformed, Dan," Sifu quickly corrects. "*Will* be! Your company will change when you change. It is just a matter of making a conscious decision to look for all the things that are around us for which we should say 'Thank you.' Teach everyone to live in thanksgiving, celebration, discovery, and appreciation.

"Last week, I was flying home from Los Angeles, and I was waiting for the connecting flight to board in Chicago. I was tired of airports and airplanes—you know how it is when you travel all day. I just wanted them to hurry up and get everybody on the plane and take me home! An elderly woman sat down beside me, and she turned to me and smiled such a lovely, radiant smile. Dan, it was so beautiful! If my focus had been on myself and my circumstances, I would have missed it. She gave of herself to me. There was real love in her eyes. I told her that she had just given me a precious gift with that wonderful smile of hers.

"Watch for every opportunity to put people first, Dan, and to make other people feel special. Every human being lives in a constant state of wondering if they are appreciated. Some people hide it better than others, but everyone is thinking the same thing: they desire the appreciation, but so few people take the initiative to supply it. Dan, if you desire to become a real leader, *you* must take the initiative, and your Purpose Partners will follow your lead."

Dan's eyes cloud with worry, and he leans across the table

toward Sifu. "Sifu, I have to ask you a question, and please don't think that I haven't been paying attention to what you've been saying. I can see I've got to make dramatic changes in my leadership style. But Sifu, I'm rated by my performance. I could spend the entire day just going around our offices and retail outlets, telling people, 'Thank you,' 'I need you,' 'I believe in you,' 'I am proud of you.' Isn't that poor use of a leader's time?"

"Dan, when you invest in other people's lives", says Sifu. "And help them grow as human beings, you are also investing in, and contributing to, your own personal growth. This is true value-added living, because when you unselfishly make a difference in other people's lives you are also adding value to your own life. Dan, there are leaders who view People First as a 'win-lose' philosophy. They see it as, 'My Purpose Partners win, because they feel better about their jobs, but I *lose*, because I am not getting my work done! You must not think of People First in terms of 'win-lose' or even 'win-win.' Think in terms of 'win-win-win.' Yes, your Purpose Partners benefit, because as you give them your belief, their own belief in themselves and their competency will grow. They become more passionate about themselves, about their work, and about others. You win, too, Dan, because as you help them to grow you will grow as a person also. Not only that, but as your organization comes to be characterized by caring Purpose Partners, your customers will come back, your organization will thrive, and *that* is exactly what you have been seeking to accomplish all along!"

Sifu reaches across the table and gives Dan's arm a playful shove. "Your Board of Directors will ask you to come give talks about how you, Dan Burton, Executive of the Year, turned your ailing company into a giant in the industry." Dan grins broadly at the idea. Sifu continues, "Seriously, Dan, People First is the right way to do business. You win, your Purpose Partners win, and the company wins. There are no losers in this equation!

"Your success, Dan, personally *and* professionally, is directly related to your ability to influence and inspire others. You said earlier that you see yourself as only a 'high-tech' person, not 'high-touch.' Dan, if you do not make personal investments in people's lives, those people will perceive that you do not really care for them as human beings, which will greatly diminish your ability to influence them to achieve your desired goals. Dan, **people willingly give you permission to lead and influence them once they become convinced how much you care for them.** The *only* way to win, Dan, personally and professionally, is to take the time to put people first!"

Dan nods his understanding. His doubts have vanished, and his eyes are clear. "I'm sorry, Sifu. That was a dumb thing to say, that I don't have time for the people. After all, I'm relying on them to make our company successful."

Sifu gives Dan his brightest smile. "There! You see? You're beginning to *think* 'People First'! And it wasn't a 'dumb' question, Dan. I have told you that I know a great many men and women who don't think they have enough time for investing in people. You had to ask the question so you would know the answer. Dan, it has been said, that 80% of the people don't think, 15% think they think, and 5% think and the thinkers are characterized by asking the best questions. Dan, you are asking the best question, I believe today that it is not that we don't know the answers, we don't even know the questions. We need great leaders to help us ask the best questions. Thank you, Dan, for asking the question."

Dan gives Sifu a grateful smile and says huskily, "You are a gracious teacher, Sifu." Then Dan brightens and he points to the peak of the pyramid that Sifu has drawn. "I'm looking forward to hearing what you have to say about this last one! It's just one word: 'Yes.' I'll bet you have mountains of distilled wisdom packed into this one word."

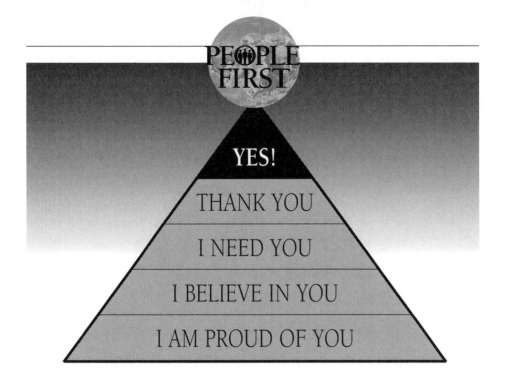

PEOPLE FIRST

YES!

THANK YOU

I NEED YOU

I BELIEVE IN YOU

I AM PROUD OF YOU

"Yes!"

Sifu nods emphatically. "'Yes' is one of the most important words any human being can hear. **'YES' stands for 'You Expect Success.'** My Sifu had a coin made up that he gave to each one of his students. He told us that success is like a two-sided coin, and he used it to teach us his whole philosophy of success. I have kept that coin all these years." Sifu deftly disengages a large silver coin from his key ring and places it in Dan's hand. It is about the size of a silver dollar. On one side of the coin, the words **Permission to Succeed** have been stamped in large block letters onto its smooth, blank face. On the other side, the words **Permission to Fail** appear in the same bold characters. Dan looks up at Sifu curiously.

"YES stands for 'You Expect Success,' Dan, because many people do not give themselves permission to succeed; they do not even *expect* to succeed. In my *kwoon*, I expect everyone to be successful. Now, I do not expect them all to succeed in the same way; they all have different gifts and talents, and each one will experience success in different degrees. However, I do expect each student to progress and improve and grow with every class."

Sifu leans forward again, and Dan listens eagerly. "It is the leader's job to create this expectancy for success. It is my job to cause them to expect to succeed. We were speaking of the first board you ever broke, and how I told you, 'Yes, Dan, you can do it! I know you will succeed. Yes! Go for it!' I want *all* my students thinking 'Yes!' I do not want negative thoughts to enter your minds that sound like, 'No, I will never do this. This is beyond my ability.'

Now, if I had instructed you to break bricks as a beginner, I would have been making it difficult for you to think 'Yes.' You would have been correct in thinking the task was impossible. But I started you off with goals I knew you could achieve with a little bit of time, knowledge, and practice. You started with the smaller, thinner, boards, and worked progressively up to bricks.

"Dan, 'Yes' is one small, solitary word, but its impact is immense and long-lasting. My Sifu drummed it into us: 'You Expect Success,' and he was always very clear in his expectations for us. He expected us to succeed in every incremental step on the journey toward earning the right to wear the black sash.

"I remember the first time I saw him do a one-legged squat. He was a big man, Dan, about 220 pounds, and he stood before us and stretched out his left leg until it was parallel to the floor. Then, keeping his left leg held out perfectly straight, he squatted on his right leg all the way to the floor, all the while keeping his left leg immobile and perfectly parallel to the floor. Then he straightened up on his right leg again." Sifu smiles that gentle smile. "He was sixty years old at the time. He was talking to us about success while he performed that squat, and he continued to talk while he did twenty repetitions on that one leg without stopping!

After completing twenty squats, he stood on his two feet and looked around the room. He asked us, 'Can any of you do this?' Well, of course, no one said a word! Our Sifu knew that we were all thinking, 'That's impossible!' We had never developed our legs to that degree.

"Do you know what he did then? He made it easy for us to think 'Yes.' He told us that the most difficult task proves to be a simple undertaking when it is broken down to its simplest unit. He told us all to stand up. Then he stood on his right leg and simply lifted his left leg off the ground and asked us, 'Can you do that?' At that point, we were all thinking, 'Yes.'

"'That is the first step to performing a one-legged squat,' he said. The next step, he told us, was to bend our right knee just a little bit, with all of our weight on that one leg. Again he was making it easy for us to believe 'Yes! I can do that.' He told us that this was the second step on the way to successfully completing a one-legged squat. He told the class, 'If you are disciplined, and go a little deeper every day, in three months time, you will be doing a one-legged squat with that opposite leg stuck straight out in front of you.' And sure enough, in three months time, I was doing one-legged squats, just as my teacher had said.

"You can see, Dan, that he was teaching us a new exercise, but he was doing far more than building strength in our legs." Sifu taps his forehead. "He was making us powerful in our minds, by teaching us to think and believe 'Yes.' He would watch us struggling to master those one-legged squats, and he never laughed at us, or said something like, 'I am an old man and I perform twenty of these. You young puppies cannot even complete one!' He used words which made us powerful. 'Yes, you can do this,' he would tell us. 'Yes, you are making good progress.' He told us that he believed in us, and that he was proud of us. He was all about 'Yes!' It cascaded from every word out of his mouth. He would say, 'Yes', to us as human beings without performing any Kung Fu. He would also say, 'Yes', to our gifts, talents, dreams, goals, and accomplishments.

"Every time he showed us a new form or technique, Dan, he *expected* us to be successful. And he taught us to expect success, as well. He showed us the goal he wanted us to achieve, and he also showed us the incremental steps we needed to master to achieve that goal.

"Dan, that lesson changed my entire outlook on life, because I began looking at any new task or skill and breaking it down into little increments and then simply gave myself permission to succeed in each of those increments. As my Sifu told us, it is a *good* thing to say 'Yes!'

"So many men and women enroll in my *kwoon* who think 'No.' I show them a new skill or challenge, and their initial thought is: 'I cannot do that. I will fail if I try that.' Somewhere along the path of life, someone told them that they are failures, that they do not make a difference. Someone threw the kill switch in their human spirit! People who are constantly told 'No' are weakened and unproductive. They are effectively dis-empowered because they are taught to think 'No,' rather than 'Yes!' Dan, you must create the kind of environment in which your family and your Purpose Partners are encouraged to think: 'Yes! What I do has *tremendous* meaning and significance. Yes! I am unique. Yes!

Other people need me. Yes! I have a lot to contribute. Yes! I make a difference. Yes! I am competent. Yes! I can make important decisions. Yes! I can flourish and tap my potential here. Yes! I have great gifts and talents."

Dan smiles, folds his arms behind his head and leans back, looking up over Sifu's head as if a particularly enjoyable movie is playing on the ceiling. "From the day I joined your *kwoon*, Sifu, you were crystal clear in communicating your expectations to me; that's how you teach all your students. You've always made it easy for me to succeed. Not that you don't make me work hard!" Dan leans forward and glares at Sifu in mock severity, and the Grandmaster grins back at him. "But when I enrolled in the *kwoon*, you didn't dangle the black sash in front of me right away and set that as my goal. That was the ultimate goal, but you brought me along step-by-step.

"You told me what was required to earn the gold sash, and how long the process would take. When I'd reached that first goal, you led me through the progression of the next five sashes, one by one. You explained the requirements for each new sash, you taught me how to measure my progress toward those goals, and you gave me constant feedback and encouragement along every step of the way.

"You celebrated my every accomplishment. Finally, after five years, I'd earned the right to wear the black sash. And during all those years, I never once felt like you'd given me a mountain that was too high to climb.

"You made it easy for me, Sifu! Every step of the way, you taught me to expect success, and to give myself permission to succeed. In fact, whenever I started thinking 'No,' you would bring my thinking back to where I believed 'Yes, I can do this!' You never criticized me, Sifu; you never once made me feel awkward or incompetent."

Sifu nods his head in acknowledgment of Dan's compliment. "Dan, gracious people are in touch with their own imperfections; therefore they do not criticize others. I have often considered printing T-shirts with the words 'Under Construction' on them and giving them to everyone I know. I would encourage them all to wear the shirt everywhere, as a constant reminder that they are still learning and growing. None of us has achieved perfection!

"People who live in criticism, condemnation, and cynicism have forgotten that they are still under construction. When a leader makes others feel incompetent, he robs them of their power as human beings. And it is not only those individuals who are hurt; the entire organization—the whole family—suffers.

"Dan, a leader makes other people powerful by imparting knowledge—knowledge of a philosophy that speaks of truth in all things, wisdom in all things, and excellence in all things. Give people the knowledge of who they are—human beings with exalted dignity, exalted worth, and exalted potential. Give them knowledge of your company's values, mission and vision, Dan, and how their individual accomplishments further the organization's objectives. Teach them how to measure their success, so that they can see when they are performing in excellence. Then set them free to accomplish great goals, and celebrate every little success! This is how you will make your Purpose Partners powerful and move beyond the preoccupation with gold to true greatness."

Dan has filled several pages of his day planner with notes. Now he slaps his pen down excitedly. "So *that's* what 'Yes' stands for! Giving people permission to succeed!"

"Not quite, Dan," Sifu replies evenly. "That is *half* of what it stands for." Sifu reaches into Dan's hand and gently turns the coin over. **"The other side of this coin reads 'Permission to fail,' and it is every bit as important to your success, and the success of your Purpose Partners, as the first side.**

"As we come to the very tip of this Pyramid of People Power, Dan, we arrive at one of the most profound lessons that my teacher ever taught me. When I was still a beginner—I had been in his *kwoon* for about five months—I became fascinated with the power of the flying side-kick. I began working very hard to master the technique. One afternoon, I was practicing the kick, and I fell. It wasn't just a little slip." Sifu smiles wryly at the memory. "I landed on my back, all sprawled out, right in the middle of the big center mat. There were about fifty students in the room, and it suddenly became very silent. Lying there on the mat, I could feel myself getting red in the face, and I started telling myself, 'You clumsy idiot! You've made a fool of yourself in front of everyone!'

"My Grandmaster walked over to me and asked, 'Why do you say bad words to yourself?'

"I told him, 'I am a failure! I have humiliated myself in front of my classmates.'

"My Sifu replied, 'Ah, you are not supposed to fail? You are the perfect student?'

"'No, Grandmaster,' I had to admit, 'I am not perfect.'

"My Sifu looked at me and said, 'Jimmy Li, you have not given yourself permission to fail.' That was the first time in my life, Dan, that I heard that expression. It had never occurred to me that we need *permission* to fail.

"My Sifu took me into his office, and there he gave me a wonderful education on the philosophy of failure. He said, 'Your mistake is an important part of your education, Jimmy. **You must learn to see failure as a valuable source of negative knowledge.**' That is when he gave me this coin which you now hold, Dan, which reads 'Permission to fail' on one side.

"My Sifu explained that in order to know what something is, you must also know what it is not. 'Negative knowledge' is simply discovering what something is not, in order to learn more about what it is. In other words, **failure teaches us how *not* to do something.** Giving yourself permission to fail is giving yourself permission to learn *from* failure. He told me to see failure as invaluable feedback.

"My Sifu began to speak about how children learn to walk. He said, 'The next time you have the opportunity, pay close attention to a young child who is just beginning to walk. You will discover that the child learns how to walk by falling down. Her mind is busily engaged in problem-solving. By falling down, she is rapidly discovering what does *not* belong to successful walking. If the child never takes the risk of falling down, or if her parents never allow her to fall, the child will never tap her potential for walking. The falling—what some might view as the child's 'failure' or 'mistakes'—is indispensable to her eventual success.'"

Sifu leans across the table, and his eyes are fairly burning into Dan's. "Dan, if we are going to succeed in *anything*, we must learn to embrace failure—to welcome it! '**Failure is inspirational dissatisfaction.**' If one is going to succeed at walking... or at Kung Fu... or in business... you must fall down. You *must* make mistakes and your dissatisfaction with them should inspire you to do better.

"Sitting in my Sifu's office that day, he told me, 'Jimmy Li, I make mistakes. I have lost tournaments. I once gave an exhibition that was attended by several hundred people, and I failed to break the bricks! But I did not hate myself or say bad words to belittle myself.' And then he said this, Dan: '**I have learned to view mistakes as stepping stones on the path to excellence, not as stumbling blocks.** If I learn from the mistake, I am discovering how *not* to do a particular task, and thus every mistake moves me closer to my desired goal.'

"As I was leaving his office that day, my Sifu said, 'Jimmy, you must not demean yourself, or fragment your sense of confidence and self-worth when you encounter failure.' He told me that the words we say to ourselves in the midst of failure define who we are as people and determine how successful we will be in our lives. Rather than using the failure as a whipping post, we must use it as a stepping stone."

Sifu leans back, but his eyes never leave Dan's face. "Dan, how do you treat yourself in the midst of failure?"

"In the *kwoon*, Sifu, I've learned to follow what you teach us. You tell us 'That's okay, you'll do better next time.' You have '**Fall down seven times, get up eight**' written on the walls!" Dan shakes his head. "But I never applied that lesson in my business or my home."

Sifu leans in toward Dan again. "Think of the immense power that you have as a leader, Dan! In the moment that a person realizes they have failed, they are the most receptive to your value judgments. They will internalize what you say to them, and carry it with them for weeks and months—possibly even for the rest of their lives. So when an employee makes an honest mistake, *especially* when it is the first time they have made that mistake, they need to hear from you that they have permission to fail. They need to carry a *positive* message away from the experience, not a negative one!

"When you are confronted with someone's failure or mistake, focus on 'What did we learn from this? How does this setback contribute to our knowledge of how to operate successfully?' Tell your

Purpose Partners, 'Yes! Negative knowledge is a crucial component of our success. We are learning and growing and moving forward. Thank you! I am so pleased that you are giving us your best efforts. I need you! You are helping our organization to move forward. I believe in you! I know you will contribute mightily to our success. I am proud of you!' *That* is the language you should employ.

"Dan, it has been rightly said that some of the most important words you will ever hear are the words you say to yourself. This is especially true in times of failure, or even when you make a simple mistake." Sifu looks piercingly at Dan. "Let me give you a helpful formula. **(E + I = SM)** In other words, **EXPERIENCE PLUS INTERPRETATION EQUALS STATE OF MIND.** "The experience itself will not break you, Dan, but it is your interpretation of the experience that can cripple you. If you berate yourself as an 'idiot' when you fail, are you likely to move forward again with confidence? I think not. Your self-talk when you fail *must* be comprised of words like, 'Yes, I am moving closer to the goal.' That is a wise interpretation of the experience.

"Dan, the words you use with your staff must be every bit as positive. Help them keep *their* self-talk positive. If you do not give your Purpose Partners permission to fail, they will *never* take risks, and without risk they will never discover the boundaries to their potential. Just as a child will never learn to walk unless he is allowed to fall, your staff will never learn to operate at their peak levels of excellence unless they are allowed to fail."

Dan is staring at Sifu, wide-eyed. "Sifu, I *never* viewed failure in that way. You're telling me that failure and mistakes are indispensable to the growth of our company, and I've got to admit to you that I've created an environment that views failure as something to be avoided at all costs. You're telling me that if I berate people when they fail, I create a fearful environment. In a fearful environment my Purpose Partners become tentative and timid. They won't take prudent risks, and our organization will *never* jump out ahead of our competitors, because we'll keep right on doing what we've always done. We won't learn and we won't grow. If I don't give the staff permission to fail, they really don't have permission to succeed." Dan hastily jots a few more notes in his day planner and looks up at Sifu. "I've got to instill a whole new philosophy about failure and mistakes in our organization," he says firmly.

"Very good, Dan!" Sifu smiles broadly. "That is correct. You can even take it a step further. Put a system in place which communicates the lessons learned from mistakes and failures throughout the entire organization, so that your Purpose Partners learn from their mistakes more quickly than your competitors do. Always make it a positive lesson; tell them that this is the way that we do *not* do things. In this way, everyone on the staff will come to understand that it is equally important to learn from our failures as well as our successes. Then your Purpose Partners will not try to hide their mistakes or shift the blame for them to somebody else. Some managers pride themselves on saying things like, 'We will not tolerate failure.' Unfortunately, you usually find an 'every man for himself' culture in that kind of workplace."

Sifu takes a sip of his coffee, then hastily sets it down. It has grown very cold. "Dan, you will enjoy great success as a leader if you always look to take the high road of excellence and create long-term, trust-based relationships. This is what I meant about 'humanizing' your organization."

Sifu is about to continue, but he stops abruptly. He has seen the excitement vanish from Dan's face, and he has once again become deeply engaged in an inspection of the silverware on the table before him. Sifu waits for a moment, then says softly, "It would appear that I have touched a nerve, my friend."

The enthusiasm has drained out of Dan's voice. "I was just thinking about that old saying... we use all the time with our sales staff and customer service reps: 'People don't care how much you know until they know how much you care.' It just occurred to me while you were talking that perhaps there is someone *else* who needs to take that message to heart." Dan looks up at Sifu. "Sifu, the staff knows I'm committed to the success of the organization, but I've never given them any reason to believe that I'm committed to *them*." Dan taps his pen on the day planner pensively. "You are absolutely right, Sifu. I'm battling a lack of trust, and *that's* why we're not moving forward like we should."

Sifu reaches across the table and gives Dan's arm an encouraging squeeze. "Dan, I am confident that you have what it takes to make the right changes. It is simply a matter of operating under the proper philosophy. **People have MMFI stamped on their foreheads for 'Make Me Feel Important,' not 'Make Me Feel Inferior.'** If you want your Purpose Partners to value the things you value, you must be committed to *them* and consistently value *them*.

"My Sifu knew all of us by name, he knew our parents—he *cared* about us! If there was anything we needed, we could go to him. He was our teacher, our psychologist, our minister, and our friend, all rolled into one. It was widely known that we could call on him at home if we needed to. And do you know, Dan, whenever he needed anything at the *kwoon*, we would drop whatever else we were doing and go do that work for him. He gave so much to us, and we were eager to give back to him.

"Not long before I left my Sifu to come to the United States, there was a fire at the *kwoon*, and one room was completely destroyed. Word spread through the city, and by mid-afternoon of the next day, two hundred students had arrived to help clean up and rebuild. My Sifu hadn't asked anyone for help; everyone just left their schools or their jobs and came to the *kwoon*. He never did hire anyone to come in and rebuild. We students were pleased to have the opportunity to demonstrate our love for him by assisting during this crisis. We pooled our talents—carpenters, electricians, painters, laborers—people came in to work at all hours of the day and night, and the job was finished in no time."

Dan has been listening closely, the pen hanging loosely in his hand, forgotten. Now Sifu taps Dan's day planner. "Dan, people go the extra mile and willingly give their highest and their best to an organization that fosters trust-based relationships. I was reminded of this just a few weeks ago, when I went to visit a man who is a senior executive at an electronics firm. He asked me to come to his office at 5:15, when the workday had just ended. Dan, the office building was deserted! There were only a few cars in the parking lot, offices were dark, everyone had gone home. I was struck by the quiet inside, and I asked a few questions. It took only a few moments to learn how discouraged that man is. He told me that the staff has no sense of loyalty to the organization."

Sifu shakes his head impatiently. "And it's no wonder! As we talked, it became clear that leadership has clearly communicated the message: 'We are not here to build relationships, we are here to get a job done.' So there *are* no Purpose Partners in that company; at 5:01, the instant they are not being paid, they scatter to their homes. No one feels any sense of connection to the organization or its goals."

Dan stares at Sifu with something like wonder in his eyes. "Sifu, I feel like I've been sleeping through most of my adult life, and you've just shaken me awake. Everything I was taught was so *different* from this! When I was taking my business courses at the university, and then again as a young executive, I was told to *avoid* close relationships with the people who worked for me. 'Don't get too close to people,' they told me. 'Stay aloof, remain distant. Don't ever let 'em get to know you on a personal level.' This is what I've heard all my life! What you are telling me is so completely removed from all that.

"And as I've been sitting here listening to you, I realize that *I am* one of those leaders you have been talking about! What was it you said? I've had money without meaning, success without significance, and shadow without substance." Dan raps his pen sharply against his day planner in an impatient gesture. "That has *got* to change!"

Sifu gives Dan an encouraging smile. "That is what the Pyramid of People Power equips you to do, Dan. You have the desire to change, and now you have the words to use to demonstrate that you really *do* put people first. You can begin today, to get to know people *as people*. **All too often we see people as 'human doings' and not as human beings.** Managers see 'Charley in Accounting, Julie in Sales,' and so on. But being precedes doing, Dan. We must not forget what it means to see people as human beings, to get to know them that way, and to speak words of encouragement into their hearts. It is amazing to me, Dan, that many leaders never discover the personal goals, life purpose, and passion of their Purpose Partners.

"Once you consistently demonstrate that you truly want to know your Purpose Partners—for who they *are*, not just what they *do*—and teach them to think 'Yes' to success, *and* 'Yes' to failure," you are living out a humanizing philosophy that taps everyone's potential and allows everyone to win."

Dan smiles and shakes his head ruefully. "It seems so odd, telling someone: 'It's okay for you to fail.' It certainly cuts against the grain of my old thinking."

Sifu nods to acknowledge the truth of Dan's statement. "**Failure should not be seen as an anomaly, something that is not a part of the success formula. It is a crucial component of success.** Dan, in the years that you have been at my *kwoon*, you have seen many students who have difficulty stepping up to try and break a board for the first time. In making the attempt, they are risking failure in front of all their classmates. There are those who prefer to live in quiet resignation, rather than risk failure. They tell themselves, 'No, this is not for me. I am not like all these other people. I don't have the ability to succeed.' If their self-talk does not change—if I, as their teacher, do not help them to change their inner dialogue—they will *never* realize their fullest potential."

Sifu reaches across the table and takes the coin Dan has been holding and lifts it to the light, turning the coin back and forth. "That is why my Sifu gave me this coin: because it represents a balanced philosophy of success. A leader will tell his or her Purpose Partners 'I expect you to succeed,' and the leader will unite that expectation of success with clear communication of the goals and measures that have been set for achieving that success. In addition to that, a leader who puts people first will recognize, celebrate, and reward every incremental accomplishment on the way toward those goals! But the leader must remember the other side of the coin. It is also vitally important to give the team permission to fail."

Sifu's eyes are boring into Dan's. "Go back and humanize your company. Put the people first, Dan. Let them know that you are more passionate about them than about profits. Playing to win is putting people first. That is taking the high road of excellence. A manager who is simply playing not to lose will put profits ahead of people. That is taking the low road of expedience—putting short-term gain ahead of long-term growth."

Now Sifu leans back from the table with an air of finality. "Dan, the choice is just that simple and just that stark. Do you want to work with money-driven performance puppets? Or passionate, meaning-driven, Purpose Partners?"

Dan is exuberant. He flips his day planner closed with a sharp *snap* and says, "I feel like you've given me a second chance to live my life! Sifu, my priorities have been all wrong. My wife and children have not been first; my Purpose Partners haven't even been on the radar screen. I've put profits first my entire life. I'm going to start putting People First in my home..." Dan's excitement is continuing to rise. "... Then I'm gonna take this philosophy into my company, and start using the Pyramid of People Power..." Dan pauses for a moment. "Shoot, I'll *teach* them the Pyramid! First I'll meet with our Executive Committee, then I'll work with all the department heads and managers and supervisors, and we'll take it through the whole organization!" Dan's mind is racing, and his eyes are very bright. Then he throws back his head and laughs with sheer exuberance. "I'd like to close our stores for an afternoon and pass out party hats and serve pizza and go around thanking everybody!"

Dan is gathering up his car keys and day planner as if he intends to charge out of the restaurant and do just that. Sifu watches silently. A smile that resembles that of a proud parent, tinged with affectionate amusement, creases his face. Suddenly Dan freezes, like a man who has just realized he has forgotten something important. He sits perfectly still for a moment, staring at Sifu. Suddenly, to Sifu's surprise, Dan's eyes begin to fill with tears.

"Sifu, thank you, thank you, *thank* you for what you've taught me today." Dan's voice is rough with emotion. "I'm so glad I found your school. I am so privileged to be given these words of wisdom. I'm going to be a good student of your philosophy." Dan's excitement is returning. "You wait and see, Sifu, as hard as I've worked to become proficient in the martial arts, I will also work to embody your philosophy. I *will* apply these principles, beginning today, and I will apply them for the rest of my life."

Suddenly Dan reaches across the table and snatches up the check for the breakfast that is lying in front of Sifu. "Don't even *think* about paying for that! And I've got the tip, too!"

"Thank you, Dan," Sifu says. Appreciation and grace, have won out over pride in his smile, which is now wider than ever.

"I can't *wait* to get to work," Dan says excitedly. He starts to rise from the table, then catches himself, and sinks back into the seat. Sifu raises a curious eyebrow. Dan's smile has vanished and he is almost businesslike. "Sifu, there's something I'd like to say to you," he begins formally. "What I want to say is... Yes!" Dan's face splits into a huge grin. "Yes! I believe in People First. Yes! I *will* make the changes I need to, both at home and at work. And thank you, Sifu. Thank you for taking all this time to help me. Thank you for all you've done for me, and for all that you do for all of us at the *kwoon*. You see, I need you Sifu. I might never have learned these things if it wasn't for your graciousness, patience and kindness. I need you because you work so hard to help me grow. You are a true model of servanthood leadership, and I need you if I'm going to keep growing."

Dan's eyes are beginning to dance with delight. "I believe in you, Sifu. I've always trusted you and respected you, but today you've shared the depth of your being with me, your philosophy of People First, and I believe in you more than ever! I believe you are a wise man and a man who shows great strength in his humility. And I am proud of you Sifu. I'm proud to have this wonderful opportunity to be taught by the finest martial artist in the world. I'm proud to be able to call you my Kung Fu Grandmaster, my mentor, and my **devoted** friend."

Sifu's laughter is unrestrained, joyous, and he claps his hands together. "You *are* a good student! You have already mastered the Pyramid of People Power! I expect to hear great things from you in the very near future."

Once again, Dan is serious. He reaches his hand across the table and takes Sifu's hand in a firm grip. "Thank you, Sifu. Thank you so very much."

"You are very welcome, my friend. I am proud of *you*, Dan. I believe you are going to make People First come alive in your home and in your business. And I am proud of you that you have been so willing to learn and to change. Shall we meet again in six months? I will be wanting to get a progress report." Sifu taps the check Dan is holding in his hand. "And another breakfast!" They both laugh.

"Absolutely!" Dan practically leaps to his feet. "I can't *wait* to get to work!"

First Things First

 *D*an is driving down the Interstate toward his office. His heart is light with new hope, and his mind is whirling with possibilities. He is planning a meeting for this afternoon with his key management personnel, and rehearsing the Pyramid of People Power in his mind. He is also weighing options for some sort of informal celebration with the staff. The comment to Sifu about "pizza and party hats" had been tossed out with little forethought, but it increasingly seems like a good idea.

Dan's eyes widen in sudden realization. *You're doing it again,* his inner voice chides him. *You walked away from that breakfast, and where did your thoughts go first? Straight to the job! Didn't you listen to anything that Sifu was saying?* "Yes," Dan says aloud, and then grins to hear himself using a Pyramid word. "Yes," he repeats, "I *was* listening."

Dan glances at his watch, then reaches for his cellular phone. He punches a few buttons and waits. "Hi honey, it's me," he announces. "Look, I know it's a little early, but I was hoping you'd let me treat you to lunch today ... No special occasion, it's just that there's something I wanted to talk to you about ... Everything's fine. This isn't bad news, it's good news, I hope. So whaddya say? ... Great! I'll be there in twenty minutes ... I love you, sweetheart."

Thirty minutes later, Dan and Cheryl Burton are seated in one of the city's finer restaurants. As the waitress approaches the table, Dan looks up with a wide smile. "Hello, my name is Dan, and this is my wife Cheryl. And your name is?"

The waitress gives Dan a quizzical look, provides her name, and recites the day's lunch specials and takes their drink orders. Cheryl is watching Dan closely. "Dan, we've been married for twenty years," she says cautiously. "You haven't taken me to lunch in years. And I've *never* seen you speak to a server that way before. Are you sure everything is alright?"

Dan chuckles. *I guess it may take some time for people to get used to the "new" Dan,* he thinks. He reaches across the table and takes

Cheryl's hands in his. "Honey, there's absolutely nothing wrong. In fact, I haven't felt so good in a long, long time. Cheryl, you know the breakfast I had scheduled with Sifu Li? Well, I've just come from there."

Cheryl's eyebrows arch in surprise. Dan has never been one for extended social contact. "I know," Dan acknowledges, "it's not like me, but this was perhaps the most profitable morning I've ever spent. Honey, I feel like I just woke up from a very long, deep sleep. Sifu held up a mirror and made me look at my reflection ... and I didn't like what I saw there. But I've learned that the wounds from a friend are faithful, and I'm grateful for that."

Dan hesitates for a moment, gathering his thoughts. He clasps Cheryl's hands even tighter and looks directly into her eyes. "What I saw today is that I've been an absentee husband and an absentee father for an awfully long time. I've taken you for granted, Cheryl, and I have completely failed to support you in all that you have done to build our family."

Cheryl stares at Dan, wide-eyed. She would have been much less surprised if Dan had told her that he had filed for a divorce! Her mouth moves, but for a moment no words will come. Finally she says softly, "Dan, I *have* felt like I've been all alone in this. Your family has *always* taken the back seat to your job." She stops speaking and peers into Dan's eyes. This is not the first time she has said these things, and she fully expects to see anger and flinty resistance etched deeply across Dan's face, but to her amazement, he is nodding his head.

"Honey," Dan says in a low voice, "I can't deny what you're saying. It's all true."

Cheryl speaks slowly, cautiously, certain that Dan will interrupt her at any moment with furious denials. "Marcy and David need you now more than ever, Dan ... there's so much in this world that seems to be aimed at destroying teenagers ... drugs, alcohol, AIDS... I read the other day that suicide is one of the leading causes of death among teenagers!" Cheryl gives Dan another searching look, and the pain she sees in his eyes causes her voice to soften. "I think the kids are okay, but Marcy doesn't talk to me much anymore. She needs you, Dan, but you've spent so much time at the office these last few years it seems like you're *never* home!"

Dan shifts uncomfortably in the cushioned booth. Some of his standard retorts run through his mind: *Oh yeah? Well, I suppose I should just start working a forty-hour week and we could pull the kids out of that expensive private school you like so much! How would that be, huh? ... Hey, I've given you everything you've ever wanted. We've got a beautiful home in a nice neighborhood, you drive a luxury car, you've got a closet full of expensive clothes, money put aside for college for the kids; that takes hard work!* After his conversation with Sifu, such words seem hollow and childish. So now he answers simply, "I know. Cheryl, you're right. I want to be there for you now ... and for Marcy and David."

Cheryl's lower lip trembles and her voice begins to break. "Dan, I do love you, but it's been so *hard* being your wife! We aren't a family, because you're never there to be *part* of a family. Your company has been your life, not your family, or even your faith.

"Dan, do you remember when we were first married, before Marcy and David were born, you told me how much you hated being raised by a father who was never home and never told you he loved you or that he believed in you? You *swore* you wouldn't be like your father, Dan." Two tears run down Cheryl's cheeks, but she seems not to notice. "Lately it seems like you've become *exactly* like him."

Dan nods miserably. "I know, Cheryl. I was talking about that very thing with Sifu this morning. We talked about a lot of things, and it all centered around my terrible attitude about people. Sifu told me I've been putting profits first all these years, and that I have to begin putting people first. And I see how that should be especially true with my family.

"Cheryl, I want to change and put you and the children first. I don't want to lose you, or lose my family. I love you very much, and I've been very foolish. Will you forgive me? *Can* you forgive me, and give me a second chance to make up to you and the children for all the years that I made you play second fiddle to my job?" Dan's voice is pleading. "Is it too late?"

Cheryl has been looking at Dan with something like wonder. But there is something else in her eyes, as well. Had he been present, Sifu Li would have immediately recognized the same joyful light of hope that he saw dawning in Dan's eyes earlier that day. "It's never too late to do what's right," she says quietly. "Yes, I forgive you, Dan. I have prayed to God for this day to become a reality." Suddenly, her face crumbles, and now the tears flow freely. "But I never really believed it would happen. Dan, your children need a father who takes an active role in their lives, and I need a husband who loves me more than he loves his job."

Dan can feel the tears on his own cheeks now, and he pauses in surprise. *I've cried more today than I have in the past twenty years,* he tells himself wryly. "Darling, I want to start over again. I promise: from this day forward, I *will* put you and our children first. You just got yourself a new husband."

Cheryl squeezes Dan's hands and smiles through her tears. "I'm very pleased to meet you," she says brightly. A choked sound, half-laughter and half-sob escapes from her throat.

Dan smiles at her tenderly. "Cheryl, there's something I was thinking about on the way over here that I want to share with you. Yes, honey, I do recognize that I failed in my most important responsibilities of all—to you and the kids. And yes, I really do love you and I'm *very* serious about wanting to change. Thank you, sweetheart, for trying to tell me all these years. I'm so sorry that I wouldn't listen. And thank you for hanging in there all these years, even though I was so wrapped up in my own 'stuff' that I ignored your needs and the kids' needs.

"I want you to know, Cheryl, that I need you. I need you to help me grow. I want to be a new man for you, and I need you to warn me if I start to fall back into my old patterns." Dan's voice is growing rough. "And sweetheart, I need *you*. I need your love; I need your support. I need to be able to come and talk to you. I don't think I've ever told you how much that means to me. I probably took your love for granted, Cheryl, but it's been so wonderful to be so sure of your love and faithfulness to me and our family."

Dan delighted in repeating back all five elements of the Pyramid to Sifu earlier, but as sincere as he was in praising and thanking Sifu, this is different. Now he is earnest and intense, trying to pour his heart into Cheryl's, and he is completely unaware that there is anyone else in the room except for the woman sitting across the table from him. "Cheryl, I believe in you. I told Sifu this morning that you are the glue that has held our home together. You've done a wonderful job raising Marcy and David, and you've done most of it alone. You stayed home for eight years to be with the kids, and then you went out and built a great career for yourself, and you *still* manage to give us all a wonderful home. I am proud of you, honey, because you've worked so very hard, and you are such a wonderful human being. I'm proud to have such a remarkable wife." Dan makes a quick mental review of what he has said, wanting to be sure he has forgotten nothing. "Honey, I know I should have told you all these things a long time ago, but please believe me when I say that they're from my heart."

Cheryl is looking at Dan through shining eyes, clutching a tissue in both hands. Suddenly she gets up from her seat and slides into the booth next to Dan, throwing her arms around his neck and burying her face into his shoulder. "I love you, Dan," she whispers, and her shoulders shake with sobs.

Dan hugs her back hard, and strokes her hair. "I love you, too, sweetheart. Things are going to be a *lot* different now." Both of them are completely oblivious to the curious looks from the people seated nearby.

The waitress starts to approach their table, then thinks better of it. She backs away with a soft smile...

Putting
*'People First' to Work*_____

$\mathcal{A}$t 3:30 that afternoon, fifteen men and women are gathered in the executive conference room at Dan's company. The in-house designation for this group is the "Executive Leadership Team." They are seated around a large conference table, and the table is strewn with the typical accoutrements of the business world: bottles of distilled water, coffee mugs, cellular phones, electronic organizers, and a day planner or note pad in front of each individual for note-taking. The group is speaking in low tones, and what little conversation that can be discerned follows the same theme:

"Do you know what this is all about?"

"Nope. I got a call from Mr. Burton's secretary to be here at 3:30."

"Well, *I* heard that the numbers from the latest quarterly statement are still bad. I don't imagine this is going to be pleasant. I'm sure Dan is in a *lovely* mood!"

Dan enters the room, cheerfully greeting them: "Hello everyone!" All conversation abruptly ceases. As Dan strides to the podium at the head of the table in the midst of the sudden stillness, a portion of this morning's conversation with Sifu echoes in his mind:

"Dan, have you ever met a leader that the room lights up, glows, radiates.... when he walks out of the room? ... Dan, are you a leader like that?"

"Yes, Sifu, I expect that I am."

Dan purses his lips at the memory. *Well, that's about to change,* he tells himself.

The group sees Dan's lips tighten, and they interpret it as a sign of displeasure. They wait in wary silence, expecting that this meeting, like so many in the past, will be stormy.

Dan stands at the podium and looks out at their carefully expressionless faces. "Thank you all for coming on such short notice," he begins. Silence. Dan looks around the room. *Like lambs waiting to go to the slaughter,* he thinks, and suddenly, unbidden, laughter bubbles up in his throat and escapes out into the room. "Man, you all look like you're expecting this to be bad!"

There are a few noncommittal smiles—only a few. *They're expecting to get yelled at some more,* Dan reminds himself. *"Shape up or ship out," and all that kind of junk. They're expecting the "old" Dan Burton.* Once again, Dan is surprised by the broad smile that suddenly stretches across his face. *I guess they're in for a surprise.*

"I'm sure you're expecting to discuss our latest Profit and Loss statements. I have them right here." Dan lifts a folder for all to see. There are a few knowing looks exchanged across the table. What happens next is unexpected. "You know what?" Dan swiftly places the folder in his briefcase and clicks it shut with a sharp *snap.* "We're not gonna do that at this time." Dan looks around the room again, and cannot contain another smile. The looks in the room range from surprise to wide-eyed astonishment. Roger, the Vice President of Sales, a bearded, heavy-set man in his early forties, is slack-jawed. Marcia, the Chief Financial Officer, a prim, neat woman whose hair is drawn tightly back in a neat bun is glaring at Dan over the top of her glasses, clearly outraged at his cavalier treatment of the report she has labored over so diligently.

"You've probably heard by now that the numbers aren't all that good, anyway," Dan continues. Heads nod around the room. "So we're not gonna focus on that. Today I want to focus on you.

"I had a long meeting today with a man who is the finest teacher

I have ever known. I met with him because I wanted to talk about business—*this* business. You've all sat in this room with me for meeting after meeting, and I've been beating on you about how 'The numbers say this,' and 'The customer surveys say that,' and everything they said was bad. I asked this man to help me see what's wrong. I was hoping he would share some new strategy which would help pull us out of this tailspin. Instead, he held a mirror up to my face and asked me how I liked what I saw... and I had to tell him that I didn't. I knew then that I was going to have to come in here and tell you, also."

Dan pauses for a moment, startled to hear his own voice growing rough with emotion. The room is absolutely hushed. The fifteen executives sit motionless in their chairs, watching and listening intently. "What I saw in the mirror is that I've failed to lead you as I should have. I saw that, instead of employing some new *strategy*, I need to adopt a whole new *philosophy* of how I deal with the people who work here." Dan takes a deep breath, and slowly lets it go. He has never in his life admitted a mistake or failure to a group of people. This is unfamiliar territory, but he knows he must push ahead.

"I've been telling you for years that 'The customer always comes first.' I realized today that, as important as it is to treat our customers well, there is another group of individuals that's even more important to the success of this business: you." Dan looks around the room. A few individuals are clearly puzzled; the rest of the faces are guarded and still. Marcia looks a little bored. "I learned today that the people of this organization *must* come first. I even learned a new phrase today: 'Purpose Partners.' You are my Purpose Partners, and if we're going to be successful, I must invest myself in you first. For my entire career, my focus has been on profits first, and the results have been less than spectacular... well, let's be honest, the results have been lousy. I've blamed you for those poor results, I've blamed our customer contact staff, I've pointed my finger everywhere except where it belongs—at me."

Now it is Jerry, the V.P. of Marketing, whose mouth is actually hanging open in undisguised amazement. Claudia, Director of Customer Service, has her head tilted to one side, and she peers at Dan through narrowed eyes as if examining something alien and unknown. Someone coughs, and the sound seems unnaturally loud in the frozen stillness.

Dan manages a shy smile. "It isn't easy for me to say these things to you. For years, I believed it was a sign of weakness to admit to failure. I've just come to realize that covering up for failure is an even greater weakness. **In other words, we put walls around weakness not strength**." Dan draws in another breath. "I have led you—and taught you to lead—in ways that don't bring out the best in people. I always thought that a leader's job was to direct and command and to keep everything tightly under his control. That philosophy has got to change—today, right now, right here."

Dan's voice grows stronger. "We are no longer going to rule by fear and intimidation. We are going to put people first. I know that has to begin with me." For the first time since the meeting began, Dan drops his eyes from the people in the room. He glances at the notebooks on the table in front of him. "I often tell you to take notes during these meetings. I'd like you to write down three words." Hands quickly stretch for the pens on the table. Dan senses that the group is grateful to be doing something that seems "normal" and familiar.

"**People First initiative.** That's what I want you to write down, and think about, and live, every minute of every day. I've walked around these offices and around our stores looking to catch people doing things *wrong*, instead of looking to celebrate what they are doing *right*. I've done it with all of you and with everyone else in our employ. I've been treating you as human doings and not as human beings, and, bottom line, that's why our net sales and customer service scores are down. It's the result of an impoverished leadership philosophy. That's got to change." Dan lets his eyes sweep around the room. "*We've* got to change," he adds earnestly. "We're going to put People First. No more criticism... no more condemnation... no more cynicism...no more throwing the kill switch in the human spirit."

Dan raises a cautionary finger. "Hear what I'm saying and what I'm *not* saying to you. I am *not* saying that customers aren't important and that profits don't matter any longer. Obviously, without customers we have no profits, and with no profits, none of us has a job. What I *am* saying is that we're going to talk about a realignment of priorities. From this day forward, our top priority is going to be the people of this organization. Our Purpose Partners are going to come first, before profits and before customer service. We will place our greatest emphasis on serving our internal customers first. I intend to live every day in celebration, discovery and appreciation of each one of you. You're an immensely talented group of people, and I don't tell you that anywhere near often enough."

Rick from Inventory Control, short, wiry, and balding, is the self-appointed humorist of the group. He can be counted on to insert a witticism at any time when he feels it will not draw Dan's displeasure. He takes a chance now. "Dan," he chirps, "does that mean this is a good time for me to ask you about that raise I've been wanting?"

The laughter in the room is far more hearty than the quip would normally warrant. Dan would usually be irritated at being interrupted in the middle of an important thought, but he senses that the group needed to release some tension. For the first time, a few hands reach out for coffee cups and water bottles, and some of the group sink back into the cushioned chairs. Dan grins back at Rick. "Rick, I want to give you all something that I hope you'll appreciate even more than a raise; I want to give you a workplace that you look forward to coming into every day. I want to make our workplace a *fun* place **and I want to give you a new philosophy that I believe will change all of our lives for the better.**"

Marcia, the CFO, leans back from the table with an air of resignation. Her body language is unmistakable: such talk is frivolous. Dan makes a mental note that he will need to spend some one-on-one time with Marcia to help her understand People First. "Let me say this to all of you," Dan continues. "I am proud of you. I'm proud of every one of you. We've been going through some difficult times and you have remained dedicated to trying to find the solution. *I* have been difficult, and you've been courteous to me and made every effort to do everything I've directed you to do. The fault for our difficulties lies with me, not with you. I believe in you." Again, Dan pauses to let the words sink in and let his eyes sweep around the room. Even Marcia is looking at Dan intently now.

"I believe in all of you. In the past, I've been all too quick to point out what I believed were your shortcomings. Well, this afternoon we will discuss *my* shortcomings—more accurately, the shortcomings in my leadership philosophy. And I'm confident that together we *will* get this organization turned around. I'm confident because I am so sure that you are an outstanding leadership team."

Smiles are beginning to replace the looks of amazement on a few faces. Others, like Sarah from Personnel, who has often been a target of Dan's displeasure, maintain a neutral expression. Marcia begins doodling on her legal pad.

"You see, I need you," Dan continues. "I need *you*, Marcia"—Marcia glances up quickly, startled—"to continue to keep me apprised of the exact nature of our financial situation, and to track what I believe is gonna be a dramatic turnaround." There are a few more smiles in the room. "But I need *all* of you to help me make this People First initiative a success. I need you to help me grow in this and hold me accountable to walking the talk.

"I also want to say thank you. Thank you for sticking with the company during these difficult times. Thank you for all the hard work and effort you've put into trying to make this company a success. Thank you for all the individual gifts and abilities that each of you brings to this team and to this organization. And thank you in advance for helping to make this new initiative a success."

Dan smiles at the group. "Lastly, I simply want to say 'Yes!' Yes, I believe that we will succeed. Yes, I am *serious* about living in celebration, discovery, and appreciation, and I want that to begin right here in this room. I say 'Yes' when you want to discuss any innovative suggestions, 'Yes' to your contributions, and 'Yes' to your continued growth. And I want to make it easy for you to say 'Yes' to others. In fact, when you're thinking about doing something that will put People First in this organization, I want you to think 'Yes!'"

Jerry from Marketing raises a tentative hand.

Dan nods reassuringly. "Go ahead, Jerry."

Jerry is cautious: "Dan, you've used that phrase 'People First' a few times now. Would you tell us a little more?"

"I'm glad you asked." Dan gives the room a sheepish smile. "I'm really excited about this, and I guess I'm charging ahead without explaining myself. Look, for as long as any of us can remember, I've been talking to you about 'The Bottom Line,' and profits, and customer service. What's missing from that equation?"

No one in the room seems eager to suggest that Dan has "missed" something. Suddenly a memory of Dan's own voice, thundering at a cowering junior executive who had just made a mistake flashes through Dan's mind: *"I don't pay you to think!"* Dan examines that memory with something like wonder. *How could I have ever thought I was going to get the best out of people by treating them like that?* he asks himself.

"What's missing," Dan says to the room at large, "is *people*. Our Purpose Partners." He swings quickly to Marcia. "Marcia, what are the most valuable assets on our balance sheet?"

"Our inventory and our capital assets," she answers crisply. "Products, buildings and land."

Dan slaps the podium with an open palm. "Marcia, I would have said the very same thing before this morning. But there's an asset *so* much more important, so much more vital than acreage and buildings and products: the people, our Purpose Partners! I want to state a disclaimer. When I say *our* Purpose Partners, I don't mean we own them. They are not our slaves. They freely choose to work here and they can freely choose to leave. So, if we want to retain the best Purpose Partners, we must believe that each and every human being in our employ possesses such a wealth of talent and ability, a shoreless, bottomless repository of untapped potential, that the possibilities for true excellence are virtually endless! In this room alone, this group right here, there is such *incredible* ability." Dan beams at the room at large. "That's one reason why I am so excited about our future, because I have such tremendous belief in all of you. *You* are the company. *You* are the image-bearers of this organization, not our buildings, not even the things we sell out of these buildings. *You* are the people our customers connect with, you and all the rest of our Purpose Partners. We have no idea how powerfully this company can perform if every man and woman who works here knows with certainty that we value them and we intend to celebrate them for who they are, and that they will be constantly empowered to accomplish their highest and best. Then we simply get out of their way and let them fulfill their mission.

"But here's the problem," and suddenly all the passion is gone from Dan's voice, and he walks out from behind the podium in order to position himself physically closer to the others. "With all the talent and all the ability that exists within this organization, with all the training we've provided, and with all our equipment and all the products, we haven't made it possible for our Purpose Partners to perform at their highest and their best. And here's the reason why: **Our Purpose Partners can't impart what they don't possess!** We tell them that 'the customer comes first,' but when did we ever put *them* first? We tell them to make the customer believe that they are our Number One reason for doing business, but when did we ever make our Purpose Partners feel like they are Number One? We tell them to value our customers and treat them with the utmost respect; do we value and respect our Purpose Partners? Do we treat them like they are our most important asset? Or the least?"

Dan sighs, and for a moment his shoulders slump. "I've been saying 'we,' but the blame for this rests squarely and solely on me. I haven't done any of these things with any of you in this room. Instead of telling you how proud I am of you..."—Dan pauses with each phrase to make eye contact with the people in the room—"... How much I believe in you,... how much I need you if we are going to succeed... instead of stopping to say 'Thank you'... instead of saying 'Yes,' and giving you permission to succeed and permission to fail... Instead of doing the things that a good leader should, I've been criticizing and condemning. Throughout my entire career, I believed that a manager's job was to look for things that were going wrong and correct them. So for twenty years now, I've been rebuking you and your predecessors for what you'd done wrong. I never once celebrated all the things you were doing right."

Dan's voice trails off, and for the first time, his eyes drop to the floor. As he has been speaking these words, the true import of the damage his high-command, high-control leadership style has done to the human spirit in his organization really comes home to him.

No one in the room moves a muscle. None of them has ever seen an executive display this kind of vulnerability before. Sarah is the youngest member of the group, fresh-faced, blonde, with cheerleader good looks. Now her bright blue eyes are narrowed with genuine concern. She clears her throat, then glances quickly around the room, startled at the sound of her own voice. "Mr. Burton?" she asks timidly.

Dan looks up at her and gives her a tired smile. This day has been perhaps the most emotionally draining of his life. "Call me Dan, Sarah. Dan will do just fine."

Sarah smiles. "Dan, thank you. Dan, you haven't been as bad as all that."

Dan gives her a sad smile. "Sarah, it's really nice of you to say that. Out of anyone in this room, I've probably been harder on you than anyone else, and yet you still say that. That's very gracious. But I've actually been *worse* than all that." Dan surveys the room. The momentary discouragement has passed, and his voice is growing stronger. "I have failed you as a leader. I've failed to establish trust with you or with anyone else in this organization. I haven't established trust because I haven't established that I care about any of you. If I want you to trust me, I must first be trust-*worthy*. But if you don't think I care about you, you aren't going to trust me."

Dan looks directly at Sarah. "Sarah, all you've heard from me for three years now is, 'What's wrong with these people you're hiring?!' Isn't that right?"

Sarah flushes and nods, looking self-consciously down at the table. Everyone in the room looks uncomfortable; they have all seen her eyes filling with tears.

Dan moves back behind the podium, drawing attention away from Sarah. "That's all *any* of you has heard from me: 'What's wrong with this? What's wrong with that?' I've put results ahead of you. I've put numbers and the bottom line ahead of you. And I've put customers ahead of you."

Dan is beginning to speak more rapidly, and he senses a change in the atmosphere of the room. Where before there had been open amazement and—*face it Dan*, he tells himself, *there was some skepticism, too*—every member of the group is now listening intently. Dan can feel them beginning to come on board, and this only fuels his excitement.

"So what have we been communicating to the staff? 'There's something wrong with you.' *That's* the message we've been sending them!" Several heads nod in agreement. Even Rick, the jokester, is listening closely, rubbing his chin thoughtfully. "That's what you've heard from me, and that's what you've passed on to the staff. No *wonder* our customer service scores keep dropping! Our staff is simply reflecting what I believed about them."

Dan moves back into the middle of the room again, and every eye follows him. "*That's* what I learned this morning," Dan tells them earnestly. "**Belief is the basis for behavior.** We've got to *believe* that our Purpose Partners are capable of great things before they'll ever *behave* in great ways!" Dan's fist is beginning to slap against his other palm, punching emphasis into his words. "*That's* why we're beginning this People First initiative in our organization. It begins *today*, right now. I want us *all* to become models of *high* empowerment, *high* involvement, *high* discovery. This is my commitment to you: I'm going to *celebrate* you and believe in you more than anyone else ever has. And *together*, we are going to *recognize* and *celebrate* the human spirit throughout this organization in a way that we *never* have before!"

"Yeah!!" Dan has been totally caught up in his words, and he is startled by the sudden shout that erupts from Roger. Mere moments ago, Roger had been practically goggle-eyed, staring at Dan in undisguised astonishment, but now he resembles a fan at a football game, bouncing up and down in his seat and pumping his fist. *"Yeah!"* he roars again. Without thinking, Roger begins to applaud vigorously, and to Dan's utter amazement, everyone in the room joins in the spontaneous ovation. Sarah is beaming up at Dan, making no effort to hide the tears running down her cheeks, and Jerry's eyes appear to be moist. Even Marcia is smiling and clapping, and raucous whoops begin to resound in the room. One by one, every member of the executive committee stands to their feet and applauds their leader. And now it is Dan's turn to gape in open-mouthed surprise.

After several moments, the noise in the room finally subsides, and the group sinks back into their chairs, grinning self-consciously at each other. Typically, Rick is the first to speak. "Hey Dan," he quips, "are you sure you weren't possessed by a space alien on your way here?"

This time the laughter is warm and genuine, and Dan joins in. "You know what Rick?" Dan is surprised at the sincerity he hears in his voice and feels in his heart. "I know I walked in here this afternoon a different man, and I *like* it!"

There are more cheers, laughter, and applause. When the second wave of noise has receded, Claudia speaks up. She is still smiling, and she speaks with a confidence that Dan has never heard before. "Dan, I guess you can see how much we all like this new idea. But can you give us some more specifics about how we go about doing this—putting people first?"

"You bet!" Dan is grateful to have the focus shift away from him. He moves to the large erasable board that occupies most of one wall in the conference room and picks up a marker. He has always been comfortable in the role of the teacher. "What is one of the great challenges that companies face in recruiting and retaining the best people? We can't promise that they'll be with us for the rest of their careers. The days of twenty-five years with a gold watch and a pension at the end are rapidly becoming a thing of the past. We can't offer them security. We can't even promise that they'll make the most money they ever have in their lives, but"—Dan jabs the marker at the group for emphasis—"we *can* promise them that we'll *train* them better than any other employer, and we'll *treat* them better than any company on the planet. When the alarm clock goes off, they won't say, 'Oh, no, I *gotta* go to work,' but 'Wow! I *get* to go to work!' And that attitude will start right here in this room."

Dan draws a large pyramid on the erasable board and begins to fill in the words Sifu taught him that morning: **Yes, Thank You, I Need You, I Believe in You, I Am Proud of You.** "This is called the Pyramid of People Power, and it contains some of the most powerful words in the English language."

Dan stops writing and turns to face the group. "I want every one of you to hold me responsible for using these words with each of you every day. And I want you to hold each other accountable for using these words with each other *and* with every single one of our Purpose Partners throughout this organization. There will be no more of this 'Do as I say, not as I do,' the way I've led you for all these years. From here on out, it will be 'Do as I do.' Are you all with me?"

There are nods and smiles and words of agreement. Dan smiles back at them. "Outstanding!" He turns back to the marker board. "Now, five of the most important words a human being can ever hear are: 'I am Proud of You...'"

Moving Forward

$\mathcal{T}$he next morning, Dan is seated at his desk. As is his custom, he has arrived at the office one hour before the workday begins in order to plan his day and work through his in-box before the phone starts ringing. Today he is sitting with a bright yellow legal pad in front of him. The words **People First** are written in bold letters at the top of the page. Dan is creating a list of suggestions for celebrating the staff that he hopes to review with the executive committee early next week. There is another category marked "Thank you letters and notes" on his page, and a growing list of names beneath it. Dan is enjoying the work, and is so engrossed that he is surprised to hear a light tap on the doorframe of his office. He looks up to see Marcia standing in the doorway.

"Dan, may I talk to you for a moment?"

"Of course, Marcia." Dan tries to keep confusion out of his voice. It has been years since Marcia knocked on his office door. Her standard procedure is to stride right in, often talking as she enters, and to stand imperiously over Dan's desk. Today she slips quietly into the office and motions to one of the chairs facing Dan's desk in a mute request for permission to sit and talk. More puzzled than ever, Dan nods, smiles, and makes a welcoming gesture toward the chair. Marcia sits and smoothes her skirt in a neat, unconscious gesture. She clears her throat nervously and looks around the room, avoiding Dan's eyes.

Dan waits and watches in silent wonderment. Marcia has risen to the top of a corporate structure that had been dominated for years by men. She has succeeded by being better at her job than anyone else, and by being aggressive and unafraid. While Dan has often found her to be assertive to the point of being abrasive, he has always respected her professional ability and trusted her to speak the truth as she sees it. So Dan is surprised to see her appear so hesitant and uncertain.

"Dan," she begins huskily, then clears her throat a second time. "I've been thinking a lot about the meeting yesterday." Her eyes flicker towards Dan, and he nods and smiles again, trying to put her at ease.

"Dan, when you first started talking about 'People First' and all that, I have to admit that I thought it was just so much touchy-feely hokum."

Dan chuckles. "I thought you might."

Marcia's quick smile seems to be tinged with sadness. "Well, you know me. I'm a numbers person, a bottom-line gal. I always have been. That's what I do."

"And you do it better than anyone I know," Dan says sincerely.

Again Marcia's eyes dart to Dan's. This time her fleeting smile is grateful. "Thank you. And I have always appreciated the opportunities you've given me here."

"I didn't 'give' them to you, Marcia," Dan replies firmly. "You earned every one of those opportunities."

Now Marcia meets Dan's gaze. "Thank you, Dan. Thank you." She draws in a deep breath and exhales slowly. Some of her tension appears to dissipate. "What I wanted to say to you was, when you first started talking yesterday, I thought it was... well, silly. You know, what could possibly be more important than the bottom line?"

Dan nods. "I know exactly. I'd always thought the same thing, until just recently."

"Well, I was watching you and listening to you talk..." Marcia stops, and looks at Dan as if she is seeing him for the first time. "I've never seen you like that before, Dan. You were so... human. So approachable. And the way the people in the room responded! After the meeting was over, a few of us stayed and talked, and everyone in the group is just … *galvanized*, Dan. They're so excited!"

Dan smiles broadly. "That's wonderful! Thanks for telling me that." Dan peers at Marcia curiously. "How do you feel about People First, Marcia?"

Marcia's voice is stronger now. "That's what I wanted to tell you." She gives a little chuckle. "It isn't easy for me to admit when I'm wrong, but... after watching you yesterday... Dan, I have to tell you that my respect for you as a leader just went through the ceiling. And I want you to know that I intend to do everything I can to help you make this People First initiative a success, because I believe it's the right thing to do." Marcia looks closely at Dan, wanting to be sure he understands. "I don't mean just that it will be successful. I mean it's the *right* thing to do. That's what I realized last night. We should have been treating our people this way all along."

Dan starts to correct her use of the phrase "our people," but quickly checks himself. *There's plenty of time to talk about "Purpose Partners" later*, he assures himself. *Right now, let's celebrate Marcia.* He smiles. "Thank you for coming in to tell me that. I know this represents a real stretch for your thinking. Hey, it's a stretch for *all* of us, because I hadn't been leading us in the right direction. But I need you to help me make People First a success, and I'm so happy to hear you say you're committed to it."

Marcia's smile is warm and confident. "We're headed in the right direction now." She hesitates, then smiles again and says, "I believe in you."

$\mathcal{P}$hilosophy $\mathcal{P}$recedes $\mathcal{P}$erformance _____

$\mathcal{S}$ix months have passed since the morning that Dan Burton and Sifu Li sat down to breakfast. Dan cannot remember a period of time that has passed so quickly or so pleasantly. One evening, just as he is straightening his desk prior to going home for dinner with Cheryl and the kids, Marcia appears at his office door with a manila folder in her hand.

Dan has been immensely gratified to see the new sense of spirit and unity among the Executive Leadership Team over the last six months. They have embraced People First, and diligently worked to spread the words of—and, more importantly, they have all become living examples of the Pyramid of People Power throughout the entire organization. Sarah's reports from Personnel have been overwhelmingly positive. The staff is responding eagerly to Dan's "People First initiative," and the impromptu "pizza and party hats" celebration that Dan scheduled for the entire organization one month to the day after his breakfast with Sifu generated a unanimously enthusiastic response.

No one has been a more vocal supporter of People First than Marcia, so Dan is surprised and disappointed to see a deep scowl on Marcia's face tonight. Dan knows she has been working on the quarterly reports, and he does not need to be told what the folder in her hand contains: the latest profit and loss statements and customer service scores. Marcia's voice is utterly cold: "I thought you'd want to see the results of this 'People First' business right away." She waves the folder, almost accusingly, in front of Dan's face. "Here."

Dan's heart sinks. *All the indications were that our sales figures would be improved,* he thinks plaintively. *How could I have been so wrong?* He takes the folder from Marcia and begins to read. He stops, glances back up the page, and re-reads. There is no mistake: gross sales are up twenty percent, and net profits show a corresponding increase. *That's great news,* he thinks. *What in the world is she looking so sour about?* Without looking up, Dan pulls the customer service scores. Overall customer satisfaction scores are up a whopping *forty* percent!

Dan hears an odd sound from Marcia, and looks up. Her eyes are shining with merriment, and she is desperately trying to stifle laughter. "Fooled ya!" she brays in a schoolyard, singsong voice and bursts into joyful, full-throated laughter.

His heart beginning to thump in his chest, Dan stares at the figures again. There can be no question: it has only been six months, but People First is already a massive success. He looks up at Marcia again, his elation building. He raises both arms in triumph, and only one word seems appropriate at that moment: *"Yes!!"*

What a day, Dan says to himself, *what a great day!* Suddenly Dan's smile vanishes and for the first time in weeks he looks almost pensive. *You know, there's someone who wasn't here today who should have been. I wish Sifu could have been here to hear the results of his People First philosophy.* Dan brightens, smiles. *It's time for another breakfast meeting,* he tells himself. *And soon!*

Epilogue:
The Grandmaster

$\mathcal{T}$hree days later, Sifu Li enters the same restaurant in which he had met a discouraged and dispirited Dan Burton six months earlier. Dan has asked to meet Sifu for breakfast in order to give him an update on People First. In reality, no such update is necessary. The success of the program has been readily apparent in Dan's increasingly relaxed demeanor and light-hearted attitude at the weekly Kung Fu classes.

But even Grandmasters are sometimes surprised.

As he was for their first appointment, Sifu is fifteen minutes early, but today when he enters the restaurant, it is Dan who is already seated and talking animatedly to the waitress. And he is not alone. An attractive brunette woman, in her early forties, is seated on the same side of the booth with Dan. The couple is pressed close together like a pair of teenagers. Sifu has met Cheryl Burton at a few social events at his *kwoon*, and recognizes her instantly. However, she looks much younger than he had remembered.

Dan and Cheryl see Sifu approaching and rise to greet him. Sifu smiles politely at Cheryl and extends a hand, but she brushes his hand aside and wraps both her arms around his neck in a warm embrace. Surprised, and feeling a little uncomfortable at this unexpected burst of affection, Sifu pats her back awkwardly.

"I see you two have met," Dan says dryly.

And then, still clinging to his neck, Cheryl Burton whispers in Sifu's ear, so that only he can hear: *"Thank you. Thank you so much. We've never been so happy."*

Then Cheryl releases her grip on Sifu's neck and stands back, still gripping his arms. Her eyes are very bright. "Yes!" she says to Sifu happily. "Thank you! I need you! I believe in you! I am proud of you!" They all three laugh together.

The waitress has been watching this spectacle with some curiosity. Most of her customers do not behave this way, especially at 6:45 AM! She smiles politely at Sifu. "May I get you some coffee, sir?"

Sifu clears his throat. He has been so moved by Cheryl Burton's spontaneous display of gratitude and her obvious joy that he is afraid his voice may break if he speaks.

Before Sifu can reply, Dan addresses the waitress. "Sifu, I'd like you to meet Joan." Dan smiles at Joan. "Joan, this is Sifu Li." Dan looks back at Sifu. "Joan was just telling us that she's going to school at night to become a nurse."

"Ah?" Sifu tests his voice and finds that it is working properly. He smiles politely at Joan. "I am always so impressed by men and women who have the determination to work full-time and attend school, also."

Joan smiles. "Thank you, sir. It *is* hard, but I'm sure it will pay off in the long run."

The Burtons and Sifu take their seats in the booth, and Dan continues. "Joan, you are talking to one of the most respected practitioners of the martial arts in the world today. Mr. Li is a Grandmaster of Walu Kung Fu. Not only that, he is the best teacher, and the best friend a man could ever hope to have. He's a friend who cared enough about me to show me my blind spots, and Joan, I had some *glaring* blind spots. He taught me how to begin traveling on the high road." Dan looks at Sifu with a grateful smile, then back up at Joan. "He gave me a wake-up call, and that's exactly what I needed in my life."

Joan has been listening with genuine interest. "Wow!" She looks at Sifu with a bright smile. "It sounds like you have a pretty good friend too, Mr. Li."

Sifu smiles warmly at Dan. "A good friend, and obviously a very good student. I suspect that in the world of business, people will soon be calling *him* 'Grandmaster.'" There are chuckles around the table, and Joan excuses herself to go fill their order.

Sifu gazes happily at Dan and Cheryl, snuggled together on their side of the booth. There is no question about it; they *both* look five years younger. The brooding frown that once seemed chiseled into Dan's face has vanished as if it never existed. "It is very nice to see you both looking so well," Sifu says cheerfully.

Cheryl giggles. "Sifu, it's even nicer to *feel* so well!" The two men join in the laughter.

Dan says quietly, "Sifu, I just don't know how to thank you enough. All the news from work is great. I just got the quarterly report three days ago, and there's a significant improvement—a *dramatic* improvement! My leadership team is happy, the staff is happy, our customers say that the staff seems much more polite and responsive, and the Chairman of the Board called me yesterday to tell me how pleased he is by our turnaround. The word he used was 'thrilled.'" Dan cocks his head to one side, relishing the sound of the word. "*Thrilled!* Can you imagine that? Just a few months ago, I was expecting him to call and ask for my resignation." Dan grins and shakes his head in disbelief.

Sifu nods and smiles, but Dan isn't finished. "But Sifu, there's something even more important than that. When I told Cheryl we were meeting for breakfast, she insisted on getting up at 5:30 and coming with me, so that you could *see*, instead of just hearing me tell you that our marriage..." Dan breaks off and looks tenderly at Cheryl, and Sifu feels the lump form in his throat again at the long look of unashamed love that passes between the two of them. Dan turns back to Sifu. "Our marriage is better than it's ever been. We wanted to tell you first, Sifu, that we're going to Estes Park, Colorado next month. We're going to have a second wedding ceremony and re-commit our marriage vows to each other."

"That's wonderful!" Sifu beams with genuine pleasure.

Dan says quietly, "*You* are wonderful, Sifu, you and the philosophy you taught me. Thank you. I've learned so *much* from you! I've learned you can get much more accomplished through caring than through coercion. I've learned that caring about others and putting people first decreases the tension and builds trust." He glances down at Cheryl again with the same tender smile. "I've learned that putting people first makes all the difference in the world."

Sifu reaches across the table and gives Dan the same two-handed salute that the students at Sifu's *kwoon* offer as a sign of respect for the teacher. Surprised, Dan salutes in return, but looks quizzically at Sifu. "You introduced me to Joan as the Grandmaster," Sifu says to Dan with a smile. "From now on, I will introduce you to others as the Grandmaster of the People First philosophy."

We would like to encourage you to share PEOPLE FIRST™ with your family, friends, and co-workers.

*I*f you are interested in purchasing PEOPLE FIRST for your organization at a group discount or simply buy extra copies for yourself, please visit our website at: **www.jacklannom.com.**

If you would like Jack Lannom to deliver his highly motivational keynote presentation *PEOPLE FIRST* at your next conference, please fax to: 954-392-1533, or, email debbie@jacklannom.com.

Lannom Inc. provides in-house Leadership Development Programs and Boot Camps for individuals based on the principles and philosophy of PEOPLE FIRST. Lannom Inc. also provides Walu Team Building Programs by Sifu Jack Lannom.

To learn more about other PEOPLE FIRST PRODUCTS and how to begin a PEOPLE FIRST PROGRAM in your company and/or to begin the first *People First* Charter in your City, fax to: 954-392-1533 or email debbie@jacklannom.com. If you would like to join a PEOPLE FIRST COMMUNITY of like-minded individuals who are actively trying to live the PEOPLE FIRST philosophy, visit us at **www.jacklannom.com** and click on the PEOPLE FIRST button.

Please Tell Us Your People First Stories!

- How has the PEOPLE FIRST philosophy changed your life?
- How are you putting it to work in your home?
  Church? Company? Community?

If this book has made a difference in your life, we would deeply appreciate you letting us know.
Please e-mail your stories to Debbie@jacklannom.com
or, return the reply card on the last page of this book.

Discover the Unlimited possibilities with the
People First Principles.

Visit our site and:

- Receive a Free E-zine and learn how to put *People First* to work in your life today.

- Share stories with other *People First* Champions

- Take the Fun Quiz to see if you are a *People First* person.

- Take the Quiz to see if you are a *People First* company.

- Download a *People First* powerpoint presentation.

- Join our *People First* Forum

- Learn 21 ways to create instant rapport with others with the *People First* principles.

- Receive a Free audio CD from the Author speaking on the Power of *People First*.

- Discover how to receive online a free Today's Motivation message from the Author 5 days a week for 52 weeks on the *People First* philosophy and much more.

- Learn how to develop *People First* Leadership skills.

- Discover how to become a *People First* certified company.

A PERSONAL MESSAGE FROM THE AUTHOR

I hope you enjoyed reading my book, PEOPLE FIRST. I really loved creating these characters so that they would come alive in your mind and make a difference in your life. My desire was to take this simple, transformational philosophy that I have used in Corporate America for over 25 years, and communicate it in story form so that these profound principles would be understood by everyone. In other words, I wanted to put the cookies on the bottom shelf. PEOPLE FIRST is all about learning how to honor, value, esteem, and respect others more highly than yourself. Can you imagine what our world would be like if everyone embraced and lived this PEOPLE FIRST philosophy? People would live happier, more productive and fulfilled lives. In an age when it is all about building the loot and passing on lunacy, I hope that you find this counter philosophy refreshing to your soul and join me in these timeless truths and begin today in a purposeful pursuit to build lives and pass on a legacy of truth, wisdom and excellence in all things.

Jack Lannom

PYRAMID OF PEOPLE POWER

Please tear out these cards, cut them apart and give them to your family, friends, and associates.

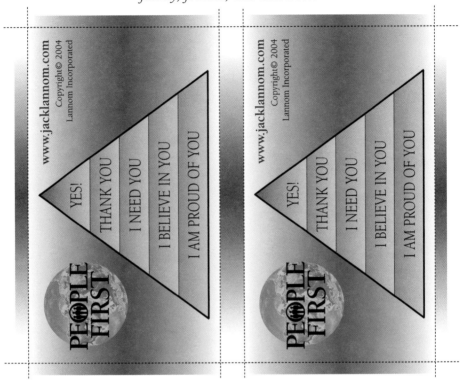

Reader/Customer Care Survey

We care about your opinions and your stories.
Please take a minute to fill out this Reader Survey card and mail it back to us.
As a special "thank you", we will send you exciting news about our upcoming books and a valuable Discount Certificate.

Name:_____

Address: _____

City:_____ ST:_____ Zip:_____

Email:_____

1. How did you find out about this book?
   ☐ Recommendation ☐ Store Display ☐ Bestseller List ☐ Online ☐ Advertising
   ☐ Catalog/Mailing ☐ Interview/Review (TV, radio, print)
2. How would you review the book? ☐ Excellent ☐ Very Good ☐ Good ☐ Fair ☐ Poor
3. Do you have a People First story to tell? If so, tell us here: _____
_____

Can we contact you to discuss: ☐ Yes ☐ No If yes, best contact information: _____
_____

4. Comments: _____
_____

Visit **www.jacklannom.com** to: See video-clips of his presentations and testimonials on Jack's development programs; to book your next event; or to order his powerful performance products.

A highlight on this site is to see Jack's upcoming programs and events! You can also send him an e-mail, sign up for his newsletter and hear a five minute motivational message from Jack 5 days a week.

Visit **www.jacklannom.com** to: See video-clips of his presentations and testimonials on Jack's development programs; to book your next event; or to order his powerful performance products.

A highlight on this site is to see Jack's upcoming programs and events! You can also send him an e-mail, sign up for his newsletter and hear a five minute motivational message from Jack 5 days a week.

Lannom Inc.
#222
2114 North Flamingo Road
Pembroke Pines, FL 33028